The Power
of the
**MASTER
MIND**

The Napoleon Hill Success Course series™

The Miracle of a Definite Chief Aim
The Power of the Master Mind
Secrets of Self-Mastery
Thrive Through Organized Thinking
Autosuggestion: Your Key to a New Life
Profiting from Failure
Winning Through Charisma
The Magic of Enthusiasm
The Sixth Sense: Your Connection to the Infinite
The Golden Rule: Your Inner Secret to Prosperity & Power

The Napoleon Hill Success Course series™

The Power
of the
MASTER MIND

By MITCH HOROWITZ

Inspired by the Teachings of
NAPOLEON HILL

An Approved Publication of the Napoleon Hill Foundation

MEDIA

Published by Gildan Media LLC
aka G&D Media
www.GandDmedia.com

First Edition: 2019
First Paperback Edition: 2021

Front Cover: Josh T. Romero

Interior design by Meghan Day Healey of Story Horse, LLC.

Library of Congress Cataloging-in-Publication Data
is available upon request

ISBN: 978-1-7225-0537-0

10   9   8   7   6   5   4   3   2   1

To Liam O'Malley,
who brought me into the Master Mind

PORTRAIT OF NAPOLEON HILL, 1908,
THE YEAR HE MET ANDREW CARNEGIE, BASED ON A PHOTOGRAPH
FROM *BOB TAYLOR'S MAGAZINE*, BY TIM BOTTA

Contents

1

What Is the Master Mind?

There is one mind common to all individual men.
Every man is an inlet to the same and to all of the same.
—RALPH WALDO EMERSON, "HISTORY," 1841

This book is about the most neglected step in Napoleon Hill's philosophy of success—and the one that he personally described as vital to the overall workability of his program: the formation and maintenance of a Master Mind group.

"Great power," Hill wrote of the Master Mind in 1937, "can be accumulated through no other principle."

Simply put, the Master Mind group is an alliance of as few as two and as many as seven members who regularly assemble to support one another's aims, plans, and ideas. The members exchange advice and counsel—and something more. Hill believed that when a group of people join together in a spirit of harmony, purpose, and mutual aid, whether aiming toward a single goal or, as is more commonly the case, assisting one another in individual goals, the participants provide not only valuable advice and ideas, but also *pool their intellects* in a manner that heightens the abilities of all of them.

This mental pooling, Hill taught, brings an additional force to their efforts—this is the Master Mind, which is an inlet of what Hill called "Infinite Intelligence." The Master Mind is Infinite Intelligence localized. (He capitalized these terms, and I have continued that practice in this book.) Hill observed:

> When two or more people coordinate in a spirit of HARMONY, and work toward a definite objective, they place themselves in a position through that alliance, to absorb power directly from the great universal storehouse of Infinite Intelligence. This is the greatest of all sources of POWER. It is the source to which the genius turns. It is the source to which every great leader turns (whether he may be conscious of the fact or not).

Transcendentalist philosopher Ralph Waldo Emerson termed this process of tapping a higher mind "The Over-Soul," the title of one of his most important essays. His concept of the Over-Soul is, in a sense, the inner key to Hill's idea.* Emerson could have been talking about the Master Mind when he wrote:

> And so in groups where debate is earnest, and especially on high questions, the company become aware that the thought rises to an equal

---

* The classic work is explored and annotated in Appendix I.

level in all bosoms, that all have a spiritual property in what was said, as well as the sayer. They all become wiser than they were.

What Makes a Group?

In his classic *Think and Grow Rich*, Napoleon Hill described the Master Mind as: "Coordination of knowledge and effort, in a spirit of harmony, between two or more people for the attainment of a definite purpose."

This coordination requires meeting at regular intervals—this is not a casual assemblage but a scheduled gathering of at least once a week. As noted, the Master Mind group consists of as few as two members, but usually no more than seven to keep things wieldy.* The group's basic function is to support and advise members in their individual goals; depending on the nature of the group, members may also offer one another prayers, meditation, and visualizations. In between meetings, members always hold one another's wishes in mind with highest esteem and encouragement. Although a Master Mind group can focus on a single goal, groups usually support each member's individual plans, purposes, and needs.

Hill wrote about two types of Master Mind groups. One type had a single goal, such as the manufacture of steel by industrialist Andrew Carnegie and his group, or the manufacture of automobiles by Henry Ford and his group. Others work together to help each member

---

* This cap at seven is Napoleon Hill's recommendation; it works well, in my experience. But this is a guideline; it is flexible based on need.

accomplish a personal goal or goals. Examples from Hill's book *The Law of Success* include the Master Mind groups established by Ford, Thomas Edison, and Harvey Firestone, and the "Big Six" in Chicago, consisting of chewing gum magnate William Wrigley and five others engaged in unrelated businesses. In this book, I focus on the latter type of Master Mind group, which works on the various goals of each member, because it can benefit many more people.

Hill emphasized that groups must gather in a spirit of harmony, personal affinity, and chemistry. There can be no divisiveness. Any kind of factionalism, conflict, or gossiping within the Master Mind will deplete its energies. If harmony prevails, the group will increase the creativity, intuition, and mental faculties of every member. But if the alliance descends into friction, it will be no more valuable than a group of strangers chatting—worth no one's time.

For this reason, you must select the members of your Master Mind group carefully, emphasizing personal affinity, shared values, and a zeal for cooperation. Any kind of pettiness, squabbling, or political arguments (always keep politics at bay) will stifle the effectiveness of the Master Mind.

Unless you are invited to join an existing group or are already part of one, you may need to assemble a group of your own. When putting together the members of your Master Mind group, you must be decisive and selective: this is not a time to idly "give someone a try" or allow someone in because you are shy about saying no. Comity and chemistry are vital—it requires choosing your colleagues with care.

At the same time, Hill insisted that you, too, must take stock of what *you* can bring to the group. He wrote:

> Before forming your "Master Mind" alliance, decide what advantages, and benefits *you* may offer the individual members of your group, in return for their cooperation. No one will work indefinitely without some form of compensation. No intelligent person will either request or expect another to work without adequate compensation, although this may not always be in the form of money.

A significant part of the "compensation" that you give other members is your vigorous participation. You are part of a mutual network. That involves not only showing up, rotating in leadership positions (as will be explored in Chapter Two), and contributing ideas to the meetings, but also to genuinely hearing what your Master Mind partners need, and not just sitting there waiting to talk. It means putting down your devices, and never allowing your Master Mind partners to hear the telltale click your fingers on a keyboard over speakerphone as you reply to emails during the meetings.

These meetings require your full attention—that is the true compensation you give your partners.

Why This Book Now?

Since Hill insisted that there is tremendous potency and possibility in a well-organized Master Mind alliance, we will spend this book exploring why that is so, how to form, run, and maintain your group, and how to get the most out of it. Many of the concepts in this book rest upon *Think and Grow Rich*—it is vital reading. If you haven't yet read *Think and Grow Rich* or if you need a refresher, you can skip to "Chapter Six, "*Think and Grow Rich*: A Master Mind Way of Life," which is a reliable encapsulation of Hill's landmark book, though not a substitute for it.

Let me say a word about why this book is needed now, and why I've called the Master Mind the most neglected step in Hill's success-building program. It is all-too-easy in today's digitally removed world to skip or avoid the vital process of forming an alliance with other people. Indeed, membership in civic and fraternal groups, from the Jaycees to the Freemasons, is down all over the country. When I was growing up in the 1970s in Queens, New York, my father was a member of the Knights of Pythias, and most neighbors had some similar affiliation—yet I know few people of my generation who belong to the fraternal orders that once dotted our nation, and brought additional cohesion to its neighborhoods. Even PTAs struggle to attract volunteers. We are no longer a nation of joiners. Unless you are a member of a twelve-step or support group—a wonderful model of a kind of Master Mind in action, as we'll explore—you are probably accustomed to a "go it alone" approach, not wanting to share intimacies with others, or to stretch your already-busy routine to accommodate yet another meeting. Many of us feel that success is a matter of inner principle and individual effort, and a group meeting seems mawkish or superfluous. I understand those feelings; I sometimes struggle with them myself.

But I can personally promise you, as a writer and historian who has studied Hill's methods for years, and who has been a dedicated member of a Master Mind group since fall of 2013, I owe a good deal of my success to this process. This step is as vital today as when Hill made the Master Mind the topic of the opening chapter of his first book, *The Law of Success*, in 1928. At that time, Hill wrote:

> In this Introduction you will find a description of a newly discovered law of psychology which is the very foundation stone of all outstanding personal achievements. This law has been referred to by the author as the "Master Mind," meaning a mind that is developed through the harmonious co-operation of two or more people who ally themselves for the purpose of accomplishing any given task.
>
> If you are engaged in the business of selling you may profitably experiment with this law of the "Master Mind" in your daily work. It has been found that a group of six or seven salespeople may use the law so effectively that their sales may be increased to unbelievable proportions.

If you think Hill was exaggerating or plying you with mere salesmanship, I direct you to the authentic and recent testimonies that appear in "Chapter Three: Master Mind Voices of Achievement," where you can hear similar, and very specific, descriptions from people who may be in work much like your own. By the time you complete this book you will understand why Hill wrote in *Think and Grow Rich*, "Compliance with this instruction is *absolutely essential*."

Today's Master Mind Practices

Another characteristic of our cyber-age is that friends and collaborators often live and work at far distances from one another. My own Master Mind group is dispersed from New Hampshire to Southern California. This is no barrier. To bridge geography and time zones, we structure things this way: Its five participants, all possessed of supportive natures, good humor, and spiritual values,* meet at a regularly designated time by conference call once each week. Not everyone is on each call each week, though full participation is the ideal we aim for. We begin by reading a short statement of principles, which is reviewed in the next chapter, and each participant then offers a piece of personal good news from the previous week. Each member then takes a turn describing his wants and needs for the week ahead. After a caller has expressed his wants and needs, each group member provides advice, ideas, encouragement, and often offers prayer or other forms of support. The call generally lasts a half-hour to 45 minutes.

For an efficient and orderly Master Mind call, it is especially important to:

---

* Although my group members come from different religious backgrounds, most coalesce around a deep-seated belief in the causative powers of the mind, a shared sense of religious faith, and a common practice of prayer, affirmations, inspirational literature, and meditation. This gives us a bedrock of familiar language, habits, and points of reference, all of which support our group identity. It is, however, unnecessary that a group be spiritual in nature, as will be explored.

1. Begin the Master Mind meeting on time;
2. commence it immediately—eschewing small talk and "meeting chatter;"
3. and cap the meeting at an hour or less, preferably no more than 45 minutes.

Now, the length of your meetings can differ depending on group size. I have participated in very complete five-person Master Mind meetings that wrapped up in a tidy 35 minutes. Such meetings don't feel rushed, but precise. Brevity, and the avoidance of "chattiness," helps prevent the drifting of attention, or clock-watching when members are pressed for time. Conducting your meetings briskly also averts feelings of friction or anxiety when one member may have greater time or flexibility, or simply more tolerance for meetings, than another. We *all* have enough meetings in our lives. Most are unnecessary. The Master Mind, by contrast, should be vital and potent; as such, its work must be well defined and precise. The Master Mind meeting, by its nature, is not a protracted experience, but a vivifying one. Members should look forward to it each week.

This collaborative alliance, if approached with purpose and harmony, will, in time, yield the kinds of extraordinary results to which Hill alluded in 1928. I can honestly say that my Master Mind group—and you will hear testimony from its own members—has proven one of the most helpful and dynamic aspects in each participant's life. Our meetings steady me when I am off course; supply fresh perspective on professional and personal issues; help me identify certain themes—both positive and negative—in my life; lend support during periods of crisis; and add buoyancy to my workweek, leaving me feeling more energized and capable after each call. Indeed, Hill noted that one may feel "lifted" for hours following a Master Mind meeting. There are also practical business benefits, in which economic or career questions are sorted out; ideas are exchanged about approaching new clients or customers; and advice is given on how to settle the inevitable frictions of the workplace.

Hill believed that the Master Mind appears behind virtually every success, whether the beneficiary knows it or not. "This form of cooperative alliance," Hill wrote, "has been the basis of nearly every great fortune."

And there is, as alluded, something greater at play.

"No two minds," Hill wrote in *Think and Grow Rich*, "ever come together without, thereby, creating a third invisible, intangible force which may be likened to a third mind." This, to him, was the "psychic phase" of the Master Mind, in which the mind may be likened to an energy which, when pooled with the intellects of others, engenders heightened intuitions, insights, hunches, and foresight. Everyone in a Master Mind group, Hill taught, gains intensified perspicacity through the conjoined subconscious minds of all the members, and the tapping of Infinite Intelligence. This produces a more vivid imaginative and mental state in which new ideas "flash" into your awareness, and you detect fresh patterns and opportunities, as well as the inner workings of things. This is also the experience of what Emerson termed the Over-Soul.

Whether you are ready to make the leap to this way of thought, I can vow to you that, from every perspective, the Master Mind will play an invaluable and practical role in your pursuit of achievement.

I once described *Think and Grow Rich* in a single sentence, which could encompass all of Hill's work: "Emotionalized thought directed toward one passionately held aim—aided by organized planning and the Master Mind—is the root of all accomplishment." (If any of my terms are unfamiliar jump to Appendix II, where I define Hill's "Sixteen Laws of Success.") This gives you a further sense of how central the Master Mind is in Hill's system.

The genius—and demand—of Hill's work is that *none* of his steps are superfluous. None are optional, even if they seem familiar, or if you think you've already done one in the past, or otherwise have it covered. Always think twice in that regard; our self-assessments often deceive or flatter us, and our habits, unless closely monitored, lean toward shortcuts and inertia.

When I encounter friends in need, I often give them a copy of *Think and Grow Rich* with the following caveat: "You must do all the exercises as if your life depends on it." If there is a "secret" to working with Napoleon Hill's ideas, that is it: nothing is "extra," and nothing—ever— is "just for beginners." When reading his work, or when rereading it, which I do at least every year, *we are all beginners*. We must approach Hill's program with fresh eyes and apply ourselves with complete dedication. That approach will aid you in more ways than you suspect.

The aim of this book is to help you perform this one vital exercise—harnessing the potency and mental strength of a Master Mind alliance—in a manner that guarantees the benefits of Hill's technique. I see the Master Mind as the gelling agent behind all of Hill's ideas, and I believe he did, too. When you properly use this force, you will have discovered one of the most important practices of your life.

2

How to Run Your
Master Mind Group

My Master Mind group meets by conference call—that
is a convenient method for our geographically dispersed
group, and for busy people in general. But you can also
meet in person, especially if your group mates are part
of your workplace or are in your general locality. In
the next chapter, you'll meet a successful Realtor and
property owner who maintains two face-to-face Master
Mind groups at real estate offices he manages in Massachusetts.

Whether face-to-face or by video or conference
call, it is important that your meetings occur in real
time to facilitate hunches and ideas, and accommodate
requests for personal help. If, for whatever reason, a
real-time meeting is temporarily impossible, you can use
other digital means to stay in touch. The one indispen-
sible factor, however, is *group harmony*. There must be

personal affinity, shared values, and chemistry. When determining your logistics and media, aim for the element of good fellowship above all else, even if it means eschewing the intimacy of a personal meeting for a digital one.

Once you have assembled your group of two to seven people, you must allow for the inevitability that certain people will come and go. It is human nature that some people commit to a meeting and then drift away, attending either intermittently or not at all. The aim should be for members to maintain their attendance as steadily as possible. If you cannot keep your word about being somewhere, you are unlikely to follow through on most things in life, including Hill's program. I urge people not to see the Master Mind as a casual engagement, like a party or coffee klatch, to be kept or broken based on convenience, all the while thinking that "others" will keep things going. If you want the personal benefits of a Master Mind alliance, just as if you want heat from a bonfire, you must tend to the fire, and your regular attendance is the only way of doing it.

It is also tempting for members to skip a meeting when everything is going well for them, and then return when they need a boost. This, too, is a mistake. In order for the group atmosphere to be there for you when you're in need, you must reliably "add logs to the fire" during periods of satisfaction and ease. What's more, others who need your support depend upon your steady participation.

Being part of a Master Mind group is an ethical commitment. The Master Mind is an intimate support group. So, once you've committed, you should be there—

and be on time. Absences or lateness demonstrate that the meetings, and the needs of your colleagues, are secondary. Hence, your attendance and timeliness should be steady, except during periods when health, family, or job requirements demand your attention elsewhere.

In case I sound a bit too severe about all this, let me also note that it is not my place to stand in judgment of another Master Minder. People have their own lives and needs, and a spirit of friendly comity and fellowship must prevail. It is a natural facet of human nature that some Master Minders will come to represent the "core" of the group, and others will participate intermittently. Some will also drift away. Accept this—and keep your group humming along harmoniously. So long as you have a quorum of two, you meet the baseline.

The Art of Persistence

Let me add one further quality to seek in potential Master Minders: persistence—but of a particular sort. "When you begin to select members for your 'Master Mind' group," Napoleon Hill wrote, "endeavor to select those who do not take defeat seriously." Hill was adamant that every striving person will experience periods of "temporary defeat," and will also encounter situations—probably many times over—where plans require a complete retooling. Hill wrote this in *Think and Grow Rich*:

> If the first plan which you adopt does not work successfully, replace it with a new plan, if this new plan fails to work, replace it, in turn with

still another, and so on, until you find a plan which DOES WORK. Right here is the point at which the majority of men meet with failure, because of their lack of PERSISTENCE in creating new plans to take the place of those which fail.

The most intelligent man living cannot succeed in accumulating money—nor in any other undertaking—without plans which are practical and workable. Just keep this fact in mind, and remember when your plans fail, that temporary defeat is not permanent failure. It may only mean that your plans have not been sound. Build other plans. Start all over again.

In the first book in the Napoleon Hill Success Course, *The Miracle of a Definite Chief Aim*, I discussed "the art of intelligent persistence." Persistence does not mean obstinacy, stubbornness, or refusal to compromise. Indeed, sticking with a situation or venture that repeatedly proves fruitless across time can, in fact, lead to permanent failure.

I once asked filmmaker David Lynch, creator of *Twin Peaks, Mulholland Drive*, and other influential and successful screen projects, how he knew he was on the right path when, as a young artist, he shifted his focus away from painting, which he had studied in college, and toward filmmaking. "I kept getting those green lights," he said.

You must, after a certain point, be getting your own "green lights"—signals that you're getting places, and that your work is hitting its mark. If not, it is time to reexamine and retool your plans. Not to give in or abandon your aim—but to fix it. Maybe you've missed something, or made an unsound assumption. This is something that your Master Mind partners are there to help you with.

A case in point occurred for me on the very afternoon in July 2017 that I am writing these words. At that time, through the help of the Master Mind, I reached a conclusion about a change I needed to make in my life. Following a discussion with my Master Mind colleague Liam O'Malley, to whom this book is dedicated, I realized that something was wrong with my professional efforts to break into television as a writer and presenter. I often have nonfiction pitches under consideration, and I have been in "hold deals" with ABC and other networks. Yet my efforts, for about ten years, had failed to bear fruit. I resolved to face the reasons why.

After speaking with my Master Mind partner Liam, I wrote these words in the margin of one of my personal copies of *Think and Grow Rich*—adjacent to Hill's passage on revising your plans, which I quoted above: "My TV plans have not been sound—I am at cross purposes. I need a new vision of what will work, and what is right/compatible with my ideals." This was a tough but liberating realization. I cannot go into the full details here, but television is a difficult place to earnestly explore—with seriousness and integrity—esoteric ideas and practical spirituality, my personal interests. The point is not to quit the medium, but to seriously rethink what venues and formats square with those values. Or, to determine—come what may—to push ahead, striving, as Rod Serling did with "The Twilight Zone," to pioneer a show, in my case, a nonfiction show dealing with the esoteric and metaphysical, which surpasses the norm. This is the kind of thing that my Master Mind colleagues have helped me think through. They understand that a dream requires grit and steady effort—they won't countenance retreat, but they also help me see new options.

To summarize, *intelligent persistence* and flexibility, not blind persistence, are the mark of a productive, successful person. Look for those qualities when seeking out your Master Mind colleagues. Your ideal partner is someone who does not grow discouraged easily, and who is also willing, without embarrassment or excessive resistance, to reconsider assumptions, beliefs, and previously settled plans.

Running Your Meeting

The basics of running your meetings should be kept very simple. I recommend that each group select a rotating Master Mind leader to chair the meeting and keep everything flowing freely. The leadership position should change weekly, with each member taking regular turns.

Here are the steps my own Master Mind group uses:

1. The weekly leader should open the meeting by reading a set of Master Mind principles, as suggested immediately after this list. (You can modify these principles to suit your needs.)

2. After reading your Master Mind principles, each member takes a turn offering a piece of personal "good news" for the past week. Members may wish

to respond to this news with ideas, encouragement, or suggestions. This is to keep the group focused on the progress of its participants, and to remain mindful of what each of you is grateful for. It's remarkable how easily we lose sight of achievements.

3. Once everybody has gone around and reported his or her good news for the previous week, it is time to state goals for week ahead. In my group, we call this "wants and needs for the week." Again, each member takes a turn naming his wants and needs for the coming week, for which he requires support, advice, prayers, etc. (Usually it is one key item, but it can be more than one.)

4. This brings us to the most vital part of the meeting: After an individual group member expresses his wants or needs for the coming week, each member in turn responds with constructive remarks, suggestions, and ideas, and possibly recommendations for meditations, visualizations, prayers, or affirmations that might help the speaker. This happens after each member speaks. So, for example, I might describe a need to meet a writing deadline—after which everyone responds. Then the next person speaks, perhaps of a sales goal, and the group responds—and so on. It is expected that during the ensuing week all Master Mind members will hold the wants and needs of each in mind. Again, depending on the nature of the group, and what members feel comfortable with, the interim period can be marked by members performing

visualizations, meditations, affirmations, and prayers for one another. Concrete economic, creative, and business advice is also offered. (All this occurs usually, but not only, during the meeting—you can stay in touch during in-between periods, a topic I'll address further).

5.   Depending on the minutes remaining, you may want to leave some time at the end of the call for questions from members of the group, who need further help on a specific topic or problem. From time to time, members may remain on the call after others depart to exchange a personal word on something.

6.   The meeting should be wrapped up within 45 to 60 minutes. An effective meeting can be as brisk as a half-hour.

The Importance of Privacy

I must say a word about confidentiality. The Master Mind meetings should be understood as a sacred fellowship, like a support group or twelve-step meeting (something related to the Master Mind phenomenon, as explored in "Chapter Four: The Master Mind and Napoleon Hill's 'Secret'"). It is vital that members expect confidentiality from the group. Master Mind meetings often touch on matters of career and finance—but can also encompass personal needs, including relationships, home life, recovery, ethical issues, and so forth. Discussions must flow freely—and privately.

You will come to intimately know your Master Mind partners. It is critical never to unduly discuss, reveal, or disclose matters in another's life to anyone outside the Master Mind group. Within the Master Mind group your discussions—which may also occur informally among members during off-times—must be entirely constructive and useful. Never descend into gossip about group members or others. It will destroy the Master Mind, and impede your self-development.

Not only are confidentiality and constructiveness essential to your group, but the general avoidance of rumor and gossip is vital to your deepest sense of self, and your existence as an ethical being. For that reason, before we look at the reading of the Master Mind principles, I ask you to consider and take the following personal pledge.

ACTION STEP:
The No-Gossip Pledge

Everything has its polar opposite. And the polar opposite of the creativity and productivity of the Master Mind group is the negative compact you slide into when you listen to or spread gossip, hearsay, and rumor.

These activities degrade your existence and your sense of self-agency, just as much as the Master Mind builds it. Each time you smear another's character, or passively listen to hearsay, you detract from your own personhood in ways that are commensurate with the gossip or rumor being spread.

You can actually feel it in the sense of exhaustion and disquiet you experience (and perhaps try to deny) each time you spread or listen to a personal rumor.

In that vein, here is an incredibly powerful step guaranteed to sharpen your mental skills and creativity, and ensure that you maintain the right kind of alliances. This one step will also energize, improve, and bring greater peace into your life. You will sleep better. You will experience greater self-respect. You will be more productive.

It comes down to two words: *Stop gossiping.*

Read those two words again. And again. Impress them upon your memory.

Acts of gossiping, tale bearing, and spreading or listening to rumors are a smog that clouds your life as much the lives of those who are defamed. "But I'm only telling the truth!" we object. Not so. Virtually every rumor that we hear or repeat is untrue, half-true, or mitigated by gravely serious circumstances of which we are unaware.

The ancient Greeks cautioned to respect your neighbor's privacy: "Zeus hates busybodies," wrote the playwright Euripides. In Judaism no sin other than murder is considered worse than tale bearing or *lashon hara*, Hebrew for "evil tongue." Modern metaphysical writers have a similar perspective: "What man says of others will be said of him," wrote New Thought author Florence Scovel Shinn. Mind-power theorist Neville Goddard taught that all talk concretizes reality, for the speaker as much as for the one spoken of.

Rejecting gossip is ever more urgent in today's world, where a huge amount of entertainment is based in smears and cruel jokes. Radio shock jocks, "reality" TV, political talk shows, snarky social media, and much of what holds our attention involves demeaning others.

By "saying no" to gossip, you not only contribute to a better home and workplace, but you *become* a nobler person. You become a leader.

Take this moment to make a personal pledge to abstain from gossip. Repeat it to yourself every morning, if necessary. Such a vow, and its follow through, will mark a turning point in your life and relationships.

Your Master Mind Principles

Each week's Master Mind meeting should open with a reading of the principles and aims of the group. This is more than a formality—it represents a commitment of each member's highest ideals, and an oath by each participant.

The military strategist Colonel Harry G. Summers (1932–1999) made an interesting point about the importance of our formal commitments. As a longtime officer, he used the example America's loss in Vietnam, which contains a piece of overlooked wisdom that could serve everyone today, whatever his personal path or pursuit.

A blunt and erudite man, Summers argued that the U.S. Army was capable of defeating North Vietnam. None of the opposing circumstances were insurmountable and, in fact, American forces almost always prevailed on the battlefield. So what, from a military perspective, went wrong?

The hard truth, Summers argued, is that the nation's political leadership never attempted to build a "moral consensus" for the war. The president never asked Congress for an official declaration of war, which many policymakers viewed as an outdated formality. But without a formal declaration, and the political process underscoring it, the public as a whole never fully supported the conflict. Hence, policymakers lacked the consent and mandate to authorize an overwhelming effort, relying instead on the chimerical (and failed) notion of a "limited war." The result was quagmire, carnage, and moral confusion.

Without a mandate, policymakers had tied their hands—and the military's. Year after year, America's political leadership authorized the army to muddle along in a half-in and half-out effort, which eroded opinion at home and frustrated commanders in the field. The missing ingredient, Summers argued, was commitment.

What works in military strategy is also what works in recovery, motivation, and self-help. You must be "all in." You must select a goal or set of principles to which you can dedicate yourself with unreserved commitment—or don't do it at all.

Hence, I believe strongly in opening each meeting with the formal reading of the Master Mind principles as an affirmation of purpose, common direction, and dedication. Liam O'Malley, who I mentioned earlier, and who first invited me into my Master Mind group, imbued this value in me. A gifted musician and salesman of the old-world kind, Liam taught me that one of the most important points and critical aspects of the weekly Master Mind is our reading of the principles. We almost never skip it.

Below are principles that are read aloud by the designed leader at the outset of each of our Master Mind meetings. These principles are adapted from life coach Bob Procter's excellent LifeSuccess consulting guidelines for forming a Master Mind group. Feel to be flexible with them, or adjust them depending on your needs and outlook. But try to capture their feel and ethics.

The Master Mind Principles
I RELEASE
I release myself to the Master Mind because I am strong when I have others to help me.

I BELIEVE
I believe the combined intelligence of the Master Mind creates a wisdom far beyond my own.

I UNDERSTAND
I understand that I will more easily create positive results in my life when I am open to looking at myself, my problems, and opportunities from another's point of view.

I DECIDE
I decide to release my desire totally in trust to the Master Mind, and I am open to accepting new possibilities.

I FORGIVE
I forgive myself for mistakes I have made. I also forgive

others who have hurt me in the past, so I can move into the future with a clean slate.

I ASK
I ask the Master Mind to hear what I really want: my goals, my dreams, and my desires, and I hear my Master Mind partners supporting me in my fulfillment.

I ACCEPT
I know, relax, and accept, believing that the working power of the Master Mind will respond to my every need. I am grateful knowing this is so.

DEDICATION AND COVENANT
I now have a covenant in which it is agreed that the Master Mind shall supply me with an abundance of all things necessary to live a success-filled and happy life. I dedicate myself to be of maximum service to God and my fellow human beings, to live in a manner that will set the highest example for others to follow, and to remain an open channel of God's will. I go forth with a spirit of enthusiasm, excitement, and expectancy.

You will find that the weekly ritual of reading the principles, shared in rotation by each week's leader, brings a sense of solidarity and enthusiasm to the meeting. It reminds you of the group's highest purpose, and subtly reinforces your faith in the agencies of group help. Take it as seriously as you would a personal pledge.

ACTION STEP:
What the Principles Mean to You

Read over the Master Mind principles above carefully. Determine how you personally relate to reach one. Do any of them need changing or adjusting? These are *your* principles; so long as you capture their overall spirit, they are flexible.

Dwell individually on each one. Think of ways that you want to live up to it, and ways that your Master Mind partners can help you. Go into your meeting feeling that when you recite or listen to these principles, they really speak to your heart, and you have a clear sense, mentally and ethically, of what these ideals mean to you.

Code Names

There are additional ways of forging group identity. My Master Mind group has a unique wrinkle: When we meet, each of its members use group names based on characters from favorite movies—figures who capture something about their hopes, ideals, and strivings. My name, for example, is "David Dunn," the lead character from M. Night Shyamalan's haunting and layered thriller, *Unbreakable*. The character resonated with me on various levels. Another one of our members uses "Balboa," since the hero of the *Rocky* movies is a source of come-from-behind inspiration for him.

When writing this book, I asked our group founder Liam: "Why did you have everyone choose movie names? And how did you choose your own name, 'Broadsword?'" He replied:

> This was a bit of fun at the outset, which turned out to take on a special meaning. I was the common friend among the original four members, and I thought it might strengthen the idea of a team of people brought together on a special mission—encouraging and supporting one another—to use "code names" on our conference call. During my recovery from a major operation, I had discovered the terrific "scrappy group bands together against impossible odds" films based on the Alistair Maclean novels *Where Eagles Dare*, *The Guns of Navarone*, and *Ice Station Zebra*. "Broadsword" and "Danny Boy" [two of the names in our group] are two of the radio-call code names used in *Where Eagles Dare*. I chose "Broadsword," and the rest followed suit with a name meaningful to them. I think the use of the names reminds us of our special role in these calls—that we are, in a very real sense, on a mission together.

Now, all this may sound a little too "Dick Tracy Decoder Ring" for you—and I'm not suggesting that this approach is for everyone. But consider whether there are ways to personalize your group, and to bring a sense of mission to what you're doing. The reading of the principles helps with that. Maybe everyone receives a token of membership, such as a meditation card, a polished stone, or framed set of principles. Maybe the group has its own anthem or song, like Todd Rundgren's "Just One Victory," Tom Petty's "I Won't Back Down," or Frank Sinatra's "That's Life." (Or maybe you're thinking I need a broadened taste in music.)

Consider this approach described by John Gilmore, the minister/spiritual director of the Open Heart Spiritual Center in Memphis, Tennessee:

> We began our Master Mind group in October of 2016. We originally began because several of us from our spiritual center, Open Heart Spiritual Center in Memphis, were either already working on our own, or about to start up ventures. We wanted to support each other. The energy from our group propelled us to make our New Year's Eve celebration an "Act As If" party. Two of the group members achieved some of their goals and ended up moving to California as a result. Another one started two businesses and is finding success with both. I began a longtime dream of being a Forex trader. We have used a few different processes, such as establishing a morning routine, and recently explored the idea of individually convening a group from history of inspirational people, much like Hill did.* . . . Overall, the process is working. We are down to four people but searching for the right folks to add.

---

* I describe this practice as used by Napoleon Hill in "Chapter Seven: Master Mind Questions and Answers."

Parties . . . role-playing . . . imagining conversations with eminent historical figures—do whatever feels *natural*, including doing nothing like this at all. The point is to make your Master Mind group *your own*, and to help everyone experience a sense of bonding, belonging, and a shared stake in one another's success.

3

Master Mind Voices of Achievement

It is important to hear directly from people involved in Master Mind groups—their experiences will become your own. In effect, reading these brief accounts begins your journey, or deepens your existing one, into the Master Mind process.

The Power of Trust

I open with someone who you'll recognize by now: Liam O'Malley, who founded my Master Mind group in 2008—and welcomed me into it in 2013. Liam is, in a real sense, responsible for this book and for the existence of our group. His comments highlight a special set of values that animate and give power to our Master Mind alliance:

I was introduced to the concept of the Master Mind in Napoleon Hill's *Think and Grow Rich*. My good friend and sales manager at the time was also a big fan of the book. We had both read the book a number of times, and would frequently refer each other to passages.

During a difficult recovery from a major operation, I had the idea of starting a Master Mind group with this friend and another who was also in sales. I did an Internet search on Napoleon Hill and Master Mind Groups, and found that a number of sites and forums had posted guidelines on how to organize a group and run meetings. These guidelines often included "The Master Mind Principles," and recommended reading them at the start of meetings.

Our Master Mind Group has evolved to the point where each member is completely open and honest about his deepest fears, failings, and anxieties—feelings and emotions that we are often unable to share with family, friends, colleagues, or professionals. We know that we will be heard but not judged. Knowing this, our members are free to express what they really want and need. They can honestly state where they need help, advice, inspiration, and encouragement, and can confidently ask the Master Mind to help them in achieving desires. This allows the other members to draw on their own experience to offer comfort, support, advice, and encouragement.

Knowing that your Master Mind partners truly want you to lead a happy and success-filled life opens your mind to new possibilities—a new way to approach a problem, a practical method to handle a challenge, or a spiritual practice to build inner strength. We are there for one another to share in our successes—many of which we relate directly to a piece of advice or encouragement received during a Master Mind call—and to share our hopes and dreams, knowing our Master Mind partners will support us in achieving them.

It is not always easy to expose yourself the way we do in our calls, but the benefits of the results—the lifting of the spirit, the tackling of the practical matter at hand, and knowing that you are in the thoughts and prayers of your partners—make it immeasurably worthwhile.

As you can detect from Liam's comments, a remarkable degree of *trust* is present in our Master Mind meetings. This is one of the reasons why it is important that members stay steady in their attendance: it creates a context and atmosphere in which participants are at liberty to speak entirely from their hearts, without embarrassment, and each member develops a baseline understanding of the other, so that a minimum degree of explanation is necessary when an issue is raised.

What's more, Liam's remarks highlight the importance of a common set of *values* among Master Minders. Within our group, those values include a personal spiritual commitment. Each member, in his own way, leads a dedicated religious life and spiritual search. This is why we can openly discuss matters that we may not always be able to share, or that may require lots of explanation and clarification, when we are dealing with professionals or friends. Some therapists or counselors take a dim view—or simply do not understand—the nature of a spiritual or inner search. Since our members are spiritually oriented, it provides a common context, and heightens intimacy and shared experiences. Again, not every Master Mind group needs to be spiritual—I address this in "Chapter Five: The Power of Peer Support" and "Chapter Seven: Master Mind Questions and Answers." But a shared set of values fosters a dynamic of mutual understanding and support.

Beyond the Ordinary

The next experience highlights what Napoleon Hill called the "psychic phase" of the Master Mind. It comes from Christopher Polak, a successful Realtor, property owner, and vice president at one of the largest real estate companies in New England. Christopher belongs to two Master Mind groups, or prosperity study groups, as he calls them, in Salem and Lynnfield, Massachusetts. He and a group member shared an experience of great personal meaning and depth. I believe that Master Minders—and all searching people—will immediately relate to it. He wrote this to me in summer of 2017:

> Last week, Tuesday, while getting ready to leave for work in the morning, I stood tying my necktie in front of the mirror attached to the bureau in my bedroom when a book with a white

spine caught my eye. It had been there among a number of books lined up on top of the bureau, along the bottom of the mirror, with stately lion bookends at each end keeping them upright. I pulled the white book out from the space it had occupied for maybe a year or so. It was a hard-cover journal called *One Good Deed a Day*. It was a gift from my prosperity teacher in Vermont, and I thought: "I'll keep this and give it to someone, someday."

Each page revealed one suggested good deed to do for that day, and a few lines on which to record your experience. 365 pages. This was a Tuesday morning, and the next morning was my weekly prosperity study group in the Salem, Massachusetts, office; so, following my teacher's lead, I decided I would give this book away in a raffle to the attending agent who guessed a number I'd pick between 1 and 20.

On Wednesday, when 10 a.m. rolled around, we had the largest weekly turnout ever—nine people including myself, when we typically have four or five regulars, sometimes up to six. We began with a round of affirmations from the current study book, and before reading the next chapter of *Think and Grow Rich* by Napoleon Hill, I paused and announced I was giving this book away to the agent who correctly guessed the number I had written down and hidden. Agents love free things, even those who make great incomes! The number I had written down was 15.

I was the last to read an affirmation, so I said that Sharon, to my left, would get to guess first. She arrived after I wrote the 15 on a sticky note, folding it over so no one would see it. Sharon immediately guessed, "15." We all laughed as I opened the sticky note and showed everyone the 15 I had written. I handed the white journal to Sharon, and described the contents to the group. Sharon opened to a random page and read aloud: "Become an organ donor." Then she said, "I'm sorry, I'm going to cry."

We waited while Sharon cleared her throat and explained that, many years ago, her sister had been ill and required an organ transplant, if she was to survive. She did receive the organ and lived seventeen healthy years as a result. It became apparent that her sister's health was failing once again, and she was hospitalized. As she continued to decline, she told Sharon that she wanted to be an organ donor as well, and asked for the forms to complete while she still could.

They got everything in place shortly before Sharon's sister's health failed further to the point where she required a ventilation machine to keep her breathing. The next day during her visit, the doctors informed Sharon there was no expectation for her sister to improve, and it was a matter of time. They also explained that once an organ donor dies, they have only a few minutes to harvest organs that can be used to save another's life. Sharon had been named the healthcare proxy, so she arrived at the painful decision to have the ventilator removed so her sister could move on. A number of minutes later, Sharon's sister took off from the runway, the doctors wheeled her body away, and retrieved what organs could be used to give life to another.

As time went on, Sharon struggled with bouts of guilt . . . "Did I do the right thing?" She would ask for a sign from her sister—any sign. But nothing seemed to come. Sharon eventually stopped asking. Then she told us, "Yesterday, Tuesday, I was in Home Depot, of all places, with my husband, and I quietly asked my sister for a sign. What kind of sign will I get in Home Depot?" Sharon now had the sign she had asked and prayed for from her sister: "Become an Organ Donor." Four words on one of 365 pages in a journal that sat on my bookcase for a year or so until Spirit moved me to pull it from the other books and give it away, with no further thought about it, when Sharon would not only need it most but also be receptive to it.

May we all remain open to our Intuition, to prompts, and to respond to them with the faith that, even though we may not always get such clear evidence, what we *do* absolutely has an effect on the world, and we are invited to play a cooperative role in this life as co-creators with the Divine.

Too Simple Not to Try

My Master Mind partner Mel Bergman has experienced a unique kind of success. Mel is a gifted musician, and a founding member of the pioneering instrumental surf-rock band The Phantom Surfers. Several years ago, Mel decided that he wanted to exit his sales job in order to dedicate himself fully to his music, specifically in the form of designing and building handcrafted, custom electric guitars.

Mel soon made a guitar called The Ether, which he personally handed to one of his musical heroes, Dave Davies, lead guitarist for The Kinks. Davies has fashioned some of the most memorable licks in rock-and-roll, and he now possesses one of Mel's axes. Mel not only transitioned his career fulltime into crafting custom guitars, but he arrived at the visionary design and production of a specialty guitar called The Wheely, customized for people who use wheelchairs. He is a pioneer in his field, and now produces an instrument that dramatically expands people's lives. Mel attributes this revolutionary change in his life to the Master Mind—affirming Hill's original insights into the potential of the process. Here is Mel's Master Mind testimony:

> To get to whatever destination you wish to go in life, would you rather row a one-man dinghy, or be a pampered passenger on a luxurious yacht? Consider the Master Mind to be your crew of expert sailors, navigating through the calm seas, as well as the storms you will surely

encounter. The concepts behind the Master Mind may seem as preposterous as a football bat, or an honest politician, but rest assured, they are more than sound. I can personally attest, as a committed skeptic, that it has changed the course of my life. For several decades, I had built guitars as a half-hearted sideline/hobby. I dreamed of one day doing it full time, but never believed with conviction that I could, or had even a ghost of a belief that it was truly possible. Once I began using the forces of the Master Mind, however, I quickly found myself being provided what I needed to transition to becoming EXACTLY what I had asked to become. Strange, but entirely true. I literally thought my way into building guitars for a living.

Whenever two or more likeminded people get together, you have a Master Mind group. It's that simple. Really. If you can suspend disbelief and give it a shot, it is inconceivable that you will not see results. Virtually anything you desire can be yours with the help of the Master Mind. Remember, thoughts are real, tangible things, and the Master Mind harnesses those thoughts and desires into real tangible results.

In fact, this tome is a direct result of the power of the Master Mind. Ten years ago, when Mitch Horowitz decided to test the power of this concept, his desire was to be a well-respected expert in the field of New Thought. As even a cursory review of his output will attest, he has more than become that. And this book was a direct result of the unlimited resources of the Master Mind providing everything needed to bring this book to you.

I can imagine what some of you are thinking: "Master Mind? Another crackpot idea that doesn't work, like all the other crackpot ideas of this type. Preposterous hocus-pocus. Pure quackery!" Sure, it does seem to stretch credulity that by talking regularly with likeminded individuals (real or imaginary!) you can realize all of your dreams and goals. But it is true. And it happened to me.

Ten years ago I set out to change the course of my profession. It was a big stretch. I had big ideas. The instructions told me to ask the Master Mind to provide me with all my desires. Oh, and make a big ask. So, with nothing to lose other than the undying regret of not even trying, I put my faith and trust in this plan. And, against all of my rational notions, lo and behold, it worked! Today I am doing exactly what I asked the Master Mind to realize for me. My thoughts became reality. Your ideas and dreams can become reality for you, too.

So many business and life plans being floated these days are unnecessarily complex. They are filled with longwinded text, complicated worksheets to fill out, and long checklists to be completed. You could add this to list *ad infinitum*. It seems like a good idea on Monday, and by Friday it is on the scrap heap.

That is the genius of the Master Mind. It is a *simple*, easy idea to execute, and it works every time. If it can work for a skeptical poltroon like me, it can certainly work for you. And if you still are unsure, try this mental ju-jitsu on for size: Ask the Master Mind to *help you* with the Master Mind!

Brothers in the Master Mind

Here is a recollection by my Master Mind partner Lou Murray, a Boston-area financial and estate planner, politics writer, and NPR commentator, who served as a delegate to the GOP convention. Although we occupy radically different political spheres, Lou is a dear and trusted friend who has prayed for my family and me, helped me in my religious search, and supported me on many occasions.

At a time of division in our country, we are brothers in the Master Mind. In Lou's story, you will find life experiences that probably reflect your own, and a comment on the sustaining power of the Master Mind throughout the workweek:

> I read *Think and Grow Rich* at a moment in time in my career when I thought I was doomed to leave the life insurance and financial planning industry. I had had several years of success, and then I found myself bogged down not just by prospects saying no, but also by life itself. A cousin who was also in sales said try Napoleon Hill.

Hill's simple, homespun prose spoke to me. I went back to it this morning in preparation for writing my thoughts on our Master Mind group. After rereading the first 10 pages or so, I think I had the same thoughts of many well-meaning believers who, after a period of being away from the Good Book, return to it and say to themselves, "Why did I ever get away from this?"

So, for me, that is the chief value of the Master Mind group: it is an aid in practicing the philosophies of Napoleon Hill, even though I haven't read the book in some time. The weekly telephone gathering is part support group, part prayer group, and part tool to foster enthusiastic persistency in all endeavors through Trust and Faith in the Master Mind.

My fellow Master Minders and I are of different political temperaments, and we are of different faiths; yet we have a special bond, and insights into one another's triumphs, desires, and goals. We have helped each other in many different ways. Our meetings are a spiritually nourishing 45-minutes of my week in the middle of a business day. To hear my Master Mind partners say as we sign off the call, "I'll be praying that you land that new contract that you have been working on—let me know how it goes," is to hear a sentiment not regularly expressed in the meeting rooms of American executives. And it is always refreshing, every week.

The Practicality of Faith

I've noted that you should tailor the tone and practices of your Master Mind group to fit the values and needs of the members. It is *your* group. Some Master Mind groups adopt a more secular, business-motivational tone, and others a more spiritual tone. As I've noted, my group tends in a spiritual direction, as that fits the outlook of its participants.

Here is testimony from my Master Mind partner Gary Jansen, a publishing executive and widely read writer on religious themes. Gary finds that the faith-based approach of our Master Mind group helps him set realistic and well-focused goals, while also retaining a sense of higher purpose:

> The Master Mind group is a weekly practical and spiritual exercise. As the Bible says, "Where two or three gather in my name, there I am." Meaning, that when the members of the Master Mind gather, we are not only sharing ideas and supporting each other's vision of a better tomorrow, we are residing in the presence of the sacred. It is what I call an Immanuel (Hebrew for "God is with us") moment. This shift in consciousness and awareness directly influences the goals each of us set in our lives, and gives us strength to overcome obstacles.
>
> Of course, God is with us in many different ways: in the love we have for our children or friends, in nature, in acts of charity we may perform. But in the Master Mind group, God,

the ultimate Master Mind, is allowing divine intelligence to be present in the ideas and dreams that are discussed during those meetings. This act of communion helps me to rationally set and refine my goals. This is where the Master Mind has benefited me most. I can often feel adrift in my purpose in life, but the Master Mind continuously brings me to center, reminding me to stay on course, and to never give up.

It seems quaint to talk about holy things. We live in a time when the hallowed is often mocked by a materialist society, which acts as if nothing exists beyond what we see in front of us. Sacred cows are often sent to the slaughterhouse, and to talk about God in the public square often brings jeers and disdain. Yet, the Master Mind is a respite from this aggression, a sacrosanct moment to be in the presence of the Holy Spirit whose job it is to guide us, and to share gifts of wisdom, understanding, counsel, fortitude, knowledge, piety, and wonder.

This is not to say that every Master Mind meeting is a revelation of great magnitude, but it is a reminder that we are never truly alone. We have partners in the form of friends who want us to succeed financially, physically, mentally, and spiritually. And we have God who wants that for us too. If God is for us—and God is—who can truly ever be against us?

Getting off the Bench

Here is my own Master Mind story. My induction into a Master Mind group helped me go from being a casual reader of Napoleon Hill's books—which gets you nowhere—to really throwing myself into Hill's ideas, with significant results:

> At an earlier point in my life, I probably would have considered the Master Mind a superfluous concept, suited to other people's lives, but not my own.
>
> For one thing, I do not take well to group or congregational spirituality (I drifted away from religious services in my mid-thirties), and I previously had some negative experiences in "encounter group" settings, in which participants are impelled to share intimacies, in some cases disclosing life details to near-strangers whose judgment you may not trust, and with whom you wouldn't necessarily share personal information in ordinary life.
>
> But when my friend Liam O'Malley invited me to join his Master Mind group in summer of 2013, I sensed a special opportunity, and immediately accepted.
>
> For me, the invitation was a chance to really apply the ideas of Napoleon Hill, which, up to that time, I had embraced in principle but failed to practice with total commitment. Soon after joining the Master Mind group, I felt moved to reread *Think and Grow Rich*—but in a spe-

cial way. This time, I told myself, I wasn't simply going to pick through the book, do a few exercises and not others, read some chapters and skim others. No. This time, I determined, I would approach the book with complete dedication, and follow step-by-step *everything* that Hill advised, including the joining of a Master Mind group. What's the point of making half a pass? If something works, it works. Find out. Full-on effort is the only way to know. Today, I often tell people that *Think and Grow Rich*, like all sound programs of self-development, will work for you—*but only if you do the exercises as if your life depends upon it.* I do not write that lightly.

With the help and encouragement of my Master Mind partners, I discovered what a full-on application of Hill's ideas could do. My career skyrocketed on several fronts: contracts arrived for books (including this ten-book series on the ideas of Napoleon Hill), as well as narration, television, and speaking appearances. The money got better and better. But those details are secondary. More importantly, I was doing what I truly wanted in my heart, and what fulfilled my Definite Chief Aim (a core Hill concept): writing and presenting on the history and practicality of metaphysical ideas in an incisive and useful way, and doing so without compromise. I felt like I had emerged from a chrysalis.

This is not to say that everything went smoothly. I met with several crises along the way, some of which are still playing out as of this writing. My Master Mind partners have helped me navigate each of them. For example, in 2014 to 2015, I was frustrated with the nature of speaking gigs that were coming my way. Some venues wanted me to speak for free (a difficult practice for someone with a family and home life), and in other cases venues were poorly run, not always keeping their commitments. For example, one prominent New Age center would send me a contract, I would deliver the agreed-upon talk, and the center would then dodge paying me. These are not uncommon issues in the alternative spiritual culture.

I agonized over how to manage the situation. With the help of my Master Minders, I reached a decision, by which I have stuck to this day: Even it means only three speaking gigs a year (and I generally do far more) I would agree only to the *right* ones. I would work with hosts who were demonstrably capable of paying (unless I'm doing it as a fundraiser), of promoting the event, and of handling logistics, including travel and hotel. Very often when a host won't pay or "invites" you to bring your own books to sell (versus ordering books themselves), nothing else is well planned, right down to the setting up of chairs.

As I alluded earlier, I also wrestle with what kinds of television pitches to make, and TV bookings to accept. These topics are under current and active consideration with my Master Mind brothers. I feel a sense of assistance and clarity whenever I gather with them. I am also charged with persistence, the quality that Napoleon Hill insisted is at the back of all success.

Part of the benefit of the Master Mind is that you and your partners, through the regular schedule of meetings and sharing of personal details, establish a rhythm, an intimacy, and a context for one another's life issues. My partners can hear and anticipate my patterns more clearly than I can, and it gives them insights into my behavior, which I don't always have the perspective to see. I also know that we are offering prayers, meditations, and visualizations all week long for one another's needs. The sense of support extends well beyond the meeting. There is simply nothing like it.

The Question of Politics

I noted in Chapter One that nothing is more likely to erode the sense of comity and fellowship that are vital to a Master Mind group than the introduction of politics. All politics are emotional. In both national and personal debates, political positions are rarely, if ever, about which policies work best; rather, politics are about what makes people *feel* psychologically safe and protected, often in an abstract sense.

"The world is ruled," Napoleon Hill wrote in 1937, on the eve of World War II, "and the destiny of civilization is established, by the human emotions."

When someone's political positions are questioned or challenged, the individual often feels that his personal sense of safety is at risk. These feelings are rarely understood as such, but this is why anger and sarcasm almost immediately appear in political disputes. The unconscious fears experienced are every bit as acute as if you were walking down a poorly lit street at night in a sketchy neighborhood and hear footsteps behind you. These intense almost instinctive reactions form the unseen emotional basis of most political debates, and they affect nearly everyone, wherever you position yourself.

Fear, accompanied by anger and vitriol, arises from the need to fend off imagined foes. With this in mind, you can be assured that if political disputes erupt during your meetings, or among members during interim periods, your group will breakdown into resentment and ineffectiveness.

Now, sometimes politics as a source of personal aspiration is unavoidable and, in fact, necessary within your group. You may find, for example, that a member of your group is participating in a political campaign (whose aims you may or may not share), and he aspires to experience success within that campaign, either as a fundraiser, organizer, activist, consultant, media figure, or even a candidate. You may encounter a Master Mind member who writes for a website or publication whose political views you share, or find distasteful or even odious. These things are part of life—they occur in Master Mind groups as they do in families.

When I was twelve years old, my father ran for Congress on the ticket of the Conservative Party in New York State. (I was proud of him. Our campaign budget: $400. A candidate for governor later told me:

"I spent that much per vote.") Several years later, at age 19, I interned for the leftwing weekly *The Nation*. This naturally created a chasm. It damaged our relationship. My father couldn't see why I would intern for a magazine whose positions he found anathema; I couldn't see why he was unable to place relationships above politics. What should you do if such things occur within your Master Mind group?

My principle is: you are there to support values and aspirations, not *positions*. You are there to ensure that a fellow Master Minder is encouraged and enabled in his highest conception of personal and ethical success. It helps to understand that even if someone is working at what you consider cross-purposes to your own political and social outlook, you would nonetheless agree that there will always be, in all human affairs, polarized sides. Your aim is not to "win"—that is not what the Master Mind is for. But, rather, you should wish that your Master Mind partner be the finest, most ethical, and clearest-thinking person on the other side, if it differs from your own. This is one of the reasons why a great deal of mutual trust must be present in the Master Mind group. Again, you're not supporting a position or an outcome—but rather encouraging an individual to rise to his personal best, which encompasses not only career success but also ethical and intellectual clarity.

A Master Mind partner once brought our group a story about a political conflict in his personal and professional life. A friend of his, he explained, was shooting a commercial for a retailer, and the friend desperately needed his help completing it. My Master Mind partner agreed to lend a hand. He was, however, deeply con-flicted. This retailer had a reputation for opposing gay rights, which not only chaffed against my friend's per-sonal ethics (and my own), but, given that he was the father of a gay child, it was an extremely painful and conflictual assignment. My Master Mind partner had already determined to contribute his fee to a gay-rights organization; so, he wasn't making any money from the deal, and was at least supporting his values indirectly. But his conscience was unassuaged.

My advice to him was this: "You are there strictly to support your friend. Life is composed of relationships. Your friend made a commitment that he is now having trouble keeping, and you are helping him—that's it. If he were marrying someone to whom you objected, and asked you to be best man, you'd agree—because you are supporting him. Sometimes we must go the distance for a friend or loved one, and frame the goal not in terms of politics, but as a matter of supporting an intimate rela-tion. That is what you're doing. It is a one-time act for a friend."

If you encounter an instance in your Master Mind group in which someone's political activity is over-whelmingly offensive to you, and you cannot, in good conscience, support that person's goals, it may be neces-sary to take a break from the group, or exit it. If tension is allowed to simmer, the group will break down. Before such steps are taken, however, I urge you to at least reflect on what I've written above; and also, in a spirit of fellowship and familial support (because the Master Mind is a kind of family), consider whether there is a way to support *the person and not the position.*

The kinds of situations I am describing may not arise in most Master Mind groups; but I feel it is necessary to at least explore these questions because such matters are increasingly common in our polarized political culture, and are only intensified by the influence of 24/7 social media. And, again, if politics is not part of your group, I suggest you avoid inviting it in, which means *keeping incidental political opinions and remarks out of your Master Mind relationships*, both during your meetings and during in-between periods when you are likely to encounter other Master Mind members.

ACTION STEP:
A Master Mind Reading List

Reading self-development books as a group builds cohesion and a special bond among Master Mind members. Certain books strengthen the experience of the group, and provide ideas for mutual support. Here are some key works that Master Mind members can read together.

1. *Think and Grow Rich* by Napoleon Hill (1937). This may seem like an obvious choice since, if you're reading this current book, chances are you're already a Hill reader and admirer. But look again. I periodically embark on a new, fresh reading of Hill's core work. I have probably done so on three or four occasions by the time of this writing. Starting fresh with *Think and Grow Rich* is

an enormously powerful exercise. If group members do this together—and if all follow the exercises as though they are encountering them for the first time—the results can be extraordinary. I provide a useful summary and refresher (not a substitute) of *Think and Grow Rich* in Chapter Six.

2. *The Science of Getting Rich* by Wallace D. Wattles (1910). The Indiana minister and social visionary provided not only outstanding principles of self-development, but also a model of ethical success. *The Science of Getting Rich* can have a wonderfully unifying effect if you experience periodic group differences, which must be resolved in order to maintain a successful Master Mind. Wattles unites all seekers in his program of principled, civic-minded, and boundlessly ambitious pursuit of one's highest aims. He reminds us that we excel as part of an interlocking chain of human relations.

3. *It Works* by R.H.J. (1926). This little pamphlet of twenty-eight pages, written anonymously by a Chicago salesman named Roy Herbert Jarrett, whose work you will encounter in "Chapter Four: The Master Mind and Napoleon Hill's 'Secret,'" contains an extraordinarily important goal-setting exercise. In three exquisitely simple steps, the author guides you in determining, maintaining, and actualizing

your most cherished aims. It seems too easy to be true, until you try it. The book's "secret" is that it induces us into a process of selection and honest reckoning of what we really want, which can help focus the aims of Master Mind members.

4. *The Secret* by Rhonda Byrne (2006). In the past, I have criticized *The Secret*. But I have gained newfound respect for the book and movie, which recently marked its tenth anniversary. At the time of this writing, I re-watched *The Secret* with my younger son, age 10, and was struck by how much I liked the movie's life-affirming values. In an era of limited attention spans, it held him rapt—and me, too. *The Secret*'s visualization program— and critics, relax, that's all it is—rests on one principle: *thoughts are causative.* I hold that to be true. But what if you just *assumed* its truth? Would it benefit your life? I think it would. Try it. *The Secret* has helped millions of people pose new questions about the possibilities of their minds, which I consider a net good. Revisiting the book and movie has helped revitalize my search.

5. *At Your Command* by Neville (1939). This slender masterpiece by Neville Goddard, who wrote under his first name, takes you to the furthest reaches of positive-mind philosophy. With aplomb and persuasiveness, Neville

argues that your *imagination is* God—and that everything you experience, including others around you, is the result of your feeling states and mental images. Neville is one of the most daring and impeccable figures in the positive-mind tradition, and is well worth discovering. He provides in-depth ideas for you and your Master Mind partners to consider, and try.

6. *Your Invisible Power* by Genevieve Behrend (1921). Behrend was the sole student of British New Thought pioneer Thomas Troward (1847-1916), who attempted to develop a comprehensive theory to explain the causal powers of the mind. Behrend, in this delightfully succinct and appealing book, explains her teacher's ideas with clarity, simplicity, and persuasion. At ninety-five readable pages, *Your Invisible Power* is one of the clearest, most engaging statements of mind-power metaphysics I know. It is a wonderful guide for your group to experience together.

7. *Alcoholics Anonymous* (1939). Conceived chiefly by AA cofounder Bill Wilson, this book distilled the ideas of philosopher William James, and a wide range of metaphysical and spiritual insights, into a practical form of healing spirituality. The first three of the famous twelve steps are a blueprint of James's idea of a "conversion experience," a vital step to personal renewal. Part of the book's genius

is that any term—anger, gambling, addiction— can be substituted for alcohol. It is arguably the most practical book ever written for people in crisis. The book has special value for Master Minders insofar as it details the power and benefits of joint work and mutual aid. Its insights are applicable to any group model. In "Chapter Five: The Power of Peer Support," I consider the affinities of twelve-step groups and the Master Mind.

4

The Master Mind and Napoleon Hill's "Secret"

In *Think and Grow Rich*, Napoleon Hill promises that a great "secret" to success is encoded throughout the book, and that this secret appears at least once in every chapter.

"The secret to which I refer," he wrote, "has been mentioned no fewer than a hundred times throughout this book. It has not been directly named, for it seems to work more successfully when it is merely uncovered and left in sight, where THOSE WHO ARE READY, and SEARCHING FOR IT, may pick it up . . . If you are READY to put it to use, you will recognize this secret at least once in every chapter."

I respect Hill's methodology, but my assumption is that if you're reading this supplemental work, you probably already possess the drive to appreciate and apply his "secret"—and if you do not, a few more indirect statements of it won't make any difference. So, I will start this chapter by supplying Hill's "secret," as I understand it, which he tied into the Master Mind process.

His secret is illustrated, sometimes surprisingly, in many anecdotes and stories in the book; but it is best on display, I think, in Hill's introductory portrait of salesman Edwin C. Barnes, who staked everything on attaining his goal of becoming a sales partner to Thomas Edison. As Hill tells it, Barnes showed up one day, unannounced and broke, at the door of Edison's laboratory in Orange, New Jersey. (You can read the abridged account in Chapter Six). Although he had ridden into town on a freight train, Barnes possessed a special and authentic state of mind. Without histrionics, and with total sincerity, he was:

1. Persistent
2. Determined
3. Certain of *exactly* what he wanted

A belief that you *can* attain what you want—backed with personal initiative, persistence, intelligent determination, and a well focused, finely honed aim, to which you hold with total consistency—is the "secret" of *Think and Grow Rich*. This marriage of absolute mental and emotional faith, and a goal toward which you work tirelessly, is the code of success.

A sound aim is often accompanied by a distinctive *fearlessness*, which is a byproduct of Hill's secret. Here is a good illustration. In 1964, the spiritual teacher Jiddu Krishnamurti delivered a series of talks to young students in India. A teen told the teacher that he feared being kicked out of his home if he violated his father's wishes and pursued a career as an engineer. You must act on your legitimate goal, the teacher urged the student, and life will rise to your demands:

> If you persist in wanting to be an engineer even though your father turns you out of the house, do you mean to say that you won't find ways and means to study engineering? You will beg, go to friends. Sir, life is very strange. The moment you are very clear about what you want to do, things happen. Life comes to your aid—a friend, a relation, a teacher, a grandmother, somebody helps you. But if you are afraid to try because your father may turn you out, then you are lost. Life never comes to the aid of those who merely yield to some demand out of fear. But if you say, "This is what I really want to do and I am going to pursue it," then you will find that something miraculous takes place.

But Hill also insisted that this fearless state of mind must be accompanied by accurate thinking, clear planning, action, and autosuggestion (the topic of a future volume in this series, and explored briefly in "Chapter Six: Think and Grow Rich: A Master Mind Way of Life"). *All of this must be amplified through the power of the Master Mind.* This point, too, appears throughout *Think and Grow Rich*, almost as frequently as the call for possessing a definite aim.

Hill's chapter on "Decision" in *Think and Grow Rich* is, for me, the golden circle where he connects his "secret" to the Master Mind. I was once rereading *Think and Grow Rich* on November 21, 2014, two days before my birthday. (As circumstances would have it now, I am now revising this segment on the same day three years later.) And I made this margin note in that chapter: "*Absolute* commitment—unwavering, with rightness at its back—is this the *power* to which he refers?" Yes—it is. But, again, *this power must be joined to the Master Mind.* In this same chapter, Hill provides the book's key example of this *joint dynamic* between the code of success and the Master Mind. He does this in his portrayal of the Committees of Correspondence, colonial America's prerevolutionary cells. Members of the Committees went on to devise and sign the Declaration of Independence, and later organized into the Constitutional Convention. I also made this note in that same day, during the same reading: "Committees of Correspondence=Master Mind." *Yes, again.*

To demonstrate exactly how Hill married his "secret" to the Master Mind, I am reproducing that key section from *Think and Grow Rich* below. It may interest you to know—as I discovered myself as of this writing—that my above-referenced margin note about "absolute commitment" first appeared at the *very end* of the passage on the Committees of Correspondence that I have selected to quote below from Hill; I made my selection of the following quoted text *before* writing the opening paragraphs of this chapter, without having realized that my designated stopping point was exactly the place where the lights went on for me about the connection between Hill's "secret" and the Master Mind.

Below is the passage from *Think and Grow Rich*, and Hill's special concluding point. Study it carefully. When Hill writes of "POWER," he is making reference to the secret to which we just referred: the harnessed abilities of mental decision. This passage is an object lesson in how a Definite Chief Aim and the agencies of the Master Mind are part of the same creative process.

The Founders and the Master Mind

> . . . the greatest decision of all time, as far as any American citizen is concerned, was reached in Philadelphia, July 4, 1776, when fifty-six men signed their names to a document, which they well knew would bring freedom to all Americans, or leave every one of the fifty-six hanging from a gallows!
>
> You have heard of this famous document, but you may not have drawn from it the great lesson in personal achievement it so plainly taught.
>
> We all remember the date of this momentous decision, but few of us realize what courage that decision required. We remember our history, as it was taught; we remember dates, and the names of the men who fought; we remember Valley Forge, and Yorktown; we remember George Washington, and Lord Cornwallis. But we know little of the real forces back of these names, dates, and places. We know still less of that intangible POWER, which insured us free-

dom long before Washington's armies reached Yorktown . . .

It is nothing short of tragedy that the writers of history have missed, entirely, even the slightest reference to the irresistible POWER, which gave birth and freedom to the nation destined to set up new standards of independence for all the peoples of the earth. I say it is a tragedy, because it is the self-same POWER which must be used by every individual who surmounts the difficulties of Life, and forces Life to pay the price asked.

Let us briefly review the events which gave birth to this POWER. The story begins with an incident in Boston, March 5, 1770. British soldiers were patrolling the streets, by their presence, openly threatening the citizens. The colonists resented armed men marching in their midst. They began to express their resentment openly, hurling stones as well as epithets, at the marching soldiers, until the commanding officer gave orders, "Fix bayonets. . . . Charge!"

The battle was on. It resulted in the death and injury of many. The incident aroused such resentment that the Provincial Assembly (made up of prominent colonists) called a meeting for the purpose of taking definite action. Two of the members of that Assembly were, John Hancock, and Samuel Adams—LONG LIVE THEIR NAMES! They spoke up courageously, and declared that a move must be made to eject all British soldiers from Boston.

Remember this—a DECISION, in the minds of two men, might properly be called the beginning of the freedom, which we, of the United States, now enjoy. Remember, too, that the DECISION of these two men called for FAITH, and COURAGE, because it was dangerous.

Before the Assembly adjourned, Samuel Adams was appointed to call on the Governor of the Province, Hutchinson, and demand the withdrawal of the British troops.

The request was granted, the troops were removed from Boston, but the incident was not closed. It had caused a situation destined to change the entire trend of civilization. Strange, is it not, how the great changes, such as the American Revolution, and the World War, often have their beginnings in circumstances which seem unimportant? It is interesting, also, to observe that these important changes usually begin in the form of a DEFINITE DECISION in the minds of a relatively small number of people. . . .

Adams conceived the idea that a mutual exchange of letters between the thirteen Colonies might help to bring about the coordination of effort so badly needed in connection with the solution of their problems. Two years after the clash with the soldiers in Boston (March '72), Adams presented this idea to the Assembly, in the form of a motion that a Correspondence Committee be established among the Colonies, with definitely appointed correspondents in each Colony. . . .

It was the beginning of the organization of the far-flung POWER destined to give freedom to you, and to me. *The Master Mind had already been organized.* [emphasis added] . . . "I tell you further, that if two of you agree upon the earth concerning anything for which you ask, it will come to you from My Father, who is in Heaven."

The Committee of Correspondence was organized. Observe that this move provided the way for increasing the power of the Master Mind by adding to it men from all the Colonies. Take notice that this procedure constituted the first ORGANIZED PLANNING of the disgruntled Colonists.

In union there is strength! The citizens of the Colonies had been waging disorganized warfare against the British soldiers, through incidents similar to the Boston riot, but nothing of benefit had been accomplished. Their individual grievances had not been consolidated under one Master Mind. No group of individuals had put their hearts, minds, souls, and bodies together in one definite DECISION to settle their difficulty with the British once and for all . . .

Meanwhile, the British were not idle. They, too, were doing some PLANNING and "Master-Minding" on their own account, with the advantage of having back of them money, and organized soldiery.

The Crown appointed Gage to supplant Hutchinson as the Governor of Massachusetts. One of the new Governor's first acts was to send a messenger to call on Samuel Adams, for the purpose of endeavoring to stop his opposition—by FEAR....

Samuel Adams had the choice of two DECISIONS. He could cease his opposition, and receive personal bribes, or he could CONTINUE, AND RUN THE RISK OF BEING HANGED!

Clearly, the time had come when Adams was forced to reach instantly, a DECISION which could have cost his life. The majority of men would have found it difficult to reach such a decision. The majority would have sent back an evasive reply, but not Adams! . . . Adams' answer: "Then you may tell Governor Gage that I trust I have long since made my peace with the King of Kings. No personal consideration shall induce me to abandon the righteous cause of my Country. And, TELL GOVERNOR GAGE IT IS THE ADVICE OF SAMUEL ADAMS TO HIM, no longer to insult the feelings of an exasperated people."

Comment as to the character of this man seems unnecessary. It must be obvious to all who read this astounding message that its sender possessed loyalty of the highest order. This is important. (Racketeers and dishonest politicians have prostituted the honor for which such men as Adams died).

When Governor Gage received Adams' caustic reply, he flew into a rage, and issued a proclamation which read, "I do, hereby, in his majesty's name, offer and promise his most gracious pardon to all persons who shall forthwith lay down their arms, and return to the duties of peaceable subjects, excepting only from the benefit of such pardon, SAMUEL ADAMS AND JOHN HANCOCK, whose offences are of too flagitious a nature to admit of any other consideration but that of condign punishment."

As one might say, in modern slang, Adams and Hancock were "on the spot!" The threat of the irate Governor forced the two men to reach another DECISION, equally as dangerous. They hurriedly called a secret meeting of their staunchest followers. (Here the Master Mind began to take on momentum). After the meeting had been called to order, Adams locked the door, placed the key in his pocket, and informed all present that it was imperative that a Congress of the Colonists be organized, and that NO MAN SHOULD LEAVE THE ROOM UNTIL THE DECISION FOR SUCH A CONGRESS HAD BEEN REACHED.

Great excitement followed. Some weighed the possible consequences of such radicalism. (Old Man Fear). Some expressed grave doubt as to the wisdom of so definite a decision in defiance of the Crown. Locked in that room were TWO MEN immune to Fear, blind to the possibility of Failure. Hancock and Adams. Through the influence of their minds, the others were induced to agree that, through the Correspondence Committee, arrangements should be made for a meeting of the First Continental Congress, to be held in Philadelphia, September 5, 1774.

Remember this date. It is more important than July 4, 1776. If there had been no DECISION to hold a Continental Congress, there could have been no signing of the Declaration of Independence.

Before the first meeting of the new Congress, another leader, in a different section of the country was deep in the throes of publishing a "Summary View of the Rights of British America." He was Thomas Jefferson, of the Province of Virginia, whose relationship to Lord Dunmore, (representative of the Crown in Virginia), was as strained as that of Hancock and Adams with their Governor.

Shortly after his famous Summary of Rights was published, Jefferson was informed that he was subject to prosecution for high treason against his majesty's government. Inspired by the threat, one of Jefferson's colleagues, Patrick Henry, boldly spoke his mind, concluding his remarks with a sentence which shall remain forever a classic, "If this be treason, then make the most of it."

It was such men as these who, without power, without authority, without military strength, without money, sat in solemn consideration of the destiny of the colonies, beginning at the opening of the First Continental Congress, and continuing at intervals for two years—until on June 7, 1776, Richard Henry Lee arose, addressed the Chair, and to the startled Assembly made this motion:

"Gentlemen, I make the motion that these United Colonies are, and of right ought to be free and independent states, that they be absolved from all allegiance to the British Crown, and that all political connection between them and the state of Great Britain is, and ought to be totally dissolved."

Lee's astounding motion was discussed fervently, and at such length that he began to lose patience. Finally, after days of argument, he again took the floor, and declared, in a clear, firm voice, "Mr. President, we have discussed this issue for days. It is the only course for us to follow. Why, then Sir, do we longer delay? Why still deliberate? Let this happy day give birth to an American Republic. Let her arise, not to devastate and to conquer, but to reestablish the reign of peace, and of law. The eyes of Europe are fixed upon us. She demands of us a living example of freedom, that may exhibit a contrast, in the felicity of the citizen, to the ever increasing tyranny."

Before his motion was finally voted upon, Lee was called back to Virginia, because of serious family illness, but before leaving, he placed his cause in the hands of his friend, Thomas Jefferson, who promised to fight until favorable action was taken. Shortly thereafter the President of the Congress (Hancock), appointed Jefferson as Chairman of a Committee to draw up a Declaration of Independence.

Long and hard the Committee labored, on a document which would mean, when accepted by the Congress, that EVERY MAN WHO SIGNED IT, WOULD BE SIGNING HIS OWN DEATH WARRANT, should the Colonies lose in the fight with Great Britain, which was sure to follow.

The document was drawn, and on June 28, the original draft was read before the Congress. For several days it was discussed, altered, and made ready. On July 4, 1776, Thomas Jefferson stood before the Assembly, and fearlessly read the most momentous DECISION ever placed upon paper. . . .

When Jefferson finished, the document was voted upon, accepted, and signed by the fifty-six men, every one staking his own life upon his DECISION to write his name. By that DECISION came into existence a nation destined to bring to mankind forever, the privilege of making DECISIONS.

By decisions made in a similar spirit of Faith, and only by such decisions, can men solve their personal problems, and win for themselves high estates of material and spiritual wealth. Let us not forget this!

Analyze the events which led to the Declaration of Independence, and be convinced that this nation, which now holds a position of commanding respect and power among all nations of the world, *was born of a DECISION created by a Master Mind, consisting of fifty-six men.* [emphasis added]

Clearly, not every Master Mind group will possess such portent, or instill in its participants such depth of vision, purpose, and fearlessness. But Hill uses this dramatic example to emphasize the invaluable role that a group *must* play in arousing wisdom, courage, supple thinking, and an appetite for intelligent endeavor and risk. There are certain heights that we simply cannot scale alone.

Although Hill emphasized the importance of decisiveness—the habit of reaching decisions quickly and firmly, and of rarely reversing them (and doing so only when new facts or radically changed conditions appear)—he also insisted that motivated individuals cannot act alone. Just as any intelligently decisive person would seek the advice of a trusted friend or colleague before making a momentous move, we need the steadying and encouraging effect of a carefully selected group to help us discern between impulse and action, between chimera and idea, between passion and intellect, between sundry information and authentic insight. As it did for the founders under the most intense historical conditions, so can a Master Mind serve us when facing the workaday realities of life.

In order to get the most out of a Master Mind group, however, you must approach this alliance with a concrete goal and sense of purpose. Do you recall the third trait of salesman Edwin C. Barnes? He was "certain of *exactly* what he wanted." Without your well-defined aim, the Master Mind has nothing to act upon. Bringing your definite aim to the Master Mind is vital to harnessing the energies of Infinite Intelligence. A goal is fuel to the fire. We now turn to this need.

The Master Mind and Your Definite Aim

Many self-development writers have observed the effects of community, relationships, and partnerships on your capacity to carry out an aim. But you must first *possess* a serious, passionately felt, and workable aim. A true aim is not a daydream or fantasy. Your aim may be bold, but it must be reachable and subject to organized planning and action. I often tell people that an authentic aim is, by definition, achievable. Otherwise, it's just a pipe dream.

In devising a genuine, meaningful aim, I often recommend an exercise from a remarkable little pamphlet I mentioned earlier called *It Works*, anonymously self-published in 1926 by a Chicago sales executive named Roy Herbert Jarrett (1874-1937). Jarrett is one of the figures I most admire in American metaphysical culture. Based on his personal experience, and years of working out his ideas in quiet experimentation, he supplied an incredibly simple, powerful exercise in goal-selection and attainment.

This exercise will help you steer around the trap of a vague or uncertain goal, and toward an aim that can be aided by the Master Mind. But I caution you: simple as this exercise may seem, it works only if you approach it, as I've written before, *as though your life depends on it*. That is my mantra. That approach is the key to every legitimate program of self-development, and it unlocks every step in Hill's philosophy. Without *total dedication*, nothing is attainable. With it, your hunger will eventually transform into opportunities for achievement and self-realization. As CS Lewis put it: "All depends on really wanting."

If you don't already know this technique, it may mark a special turning point for you. And if you do know it, I hope that what I write here will return you to it with renewed vigor. In essence, Jarrett distilled a program of creative-mind philosophy into three basic steps, which I have adapted:

1. Carefully devise a list of what you *really* want from life. This may mean working on your list for days, weeks, or even months. Write it over and over again until you feel morally certain it contains your deepest wishes.

2. Once you have your list sculpted to the absolute truth, write it down like a personal contract, and carry it with you. Read it morning, noon, and night. Think about it always. Mix your reading and thoughts with feeling; your list should arouse your fondest desires.

3. *Tell no one what you are doing* so you remain steady in your resolve. Too often we disclose our wishes hastily and foolishly to others. People often demean or dismiss the dreams of friends, coworkers, and family members, thus disrupting their equilibrium and depleting their morale. Do not let this happen to you. *Remain silent*. The Master Mind is your proper outlet.

Then, express gratitude when the results arrive.

How can such a simple exercise really work? Because it pushes us to do something that we *think* we do all time but rarely try: *honestly come to terms with our truest desires.* Really *knowing* your desires can summon energies and possibilities you didn't know existed. Most of us drift through life lazily thinking that we know what we want: a new house, a loving mate, a better job, etc. Or we are consumed by fleeting hungers, which we experience and satisfy in the space of a moment, like Isaac selling out his birthright for a bowl of pottage. But I urge you: sit down privately, in a mature and sustained manner, stripped of all convention, inhibition, and embarrassment, and ask yourself what you *really* want from life. Try these three steps. Throw yourself into them. The result will almost certainly surprise you.

Getting to the One Thing

Now, I wrote that you, like Edwin C. Barnes, must select the *one thing* for which you yearn above all else. In the steps above, I am asking you to compile a list of things. Is there a contradiction? This is where I part ways from Jarrett and cleave more closely to the ideal espoused by Napoleon Hill: You must select one Definite Chief Aim (a term Hill capitalized). You will probably notice that most things on your list converge around a certain point. You must use that knowledge to take a further step, namely: honing in on your one major life goal. That is the aim you will bring into your Master Mind group.

Take note of the experience of the world-famous mythologist Joseph Campbell (1904-1987). Just before the Great Depression, Campbell was living in New York City. Pushing thirty, the not-so-young seeker was adrift: He had no idea what he wanted to do with his life. On Sundays, Campbell attended a metaphysical church presided over by a minister named Fenwicke Holmes. Fenwicke was the brother and collaborator of Ernest Holmes, one of the architects of "the power of positive thinking," and the founder of the philosophy and magazine called *Science of Mind*. Campbell approached Fenwicke for advice. The minister gave him an exercise to discover where he should direct his energies in life: "One should jot down notes for a period of four or five weeks on the things that interest one. It will be found that all the interests tend in a certain direction." This simple technique solidified Campbell's wish to study mythology. The exercise later echoed in Campbell's widely known aphorism: "Follow your bliss."

Campbell's advice has many practical sides. I once asked a development executive in television how people avoid going crazy in such a slippery, uncertain business. In TV, promises are quickly made and broken; pitches are green-lighted and then killed—how does one cope? He said there are three types of people in creative development: 1) those who are always having great ideas, and excel; 2) those who have an incredibly thick skin, and can put up with inevitable disappointments and reversals; and 3) those who "lose it," whose hair is prematurely gray and fingernails are bitten down from stress. Of course, one ideally wants to be in the first category, in whatever profession you occupy. But the only way to be in that category is to occupy the *right* profession. The path with bliss, and for which you feel joyous passion, is that for which you are ideally suited. Only then can you have great ideas on a steady basis, and feel productive, powerful, and needed.

Is it the Right Aim?

People sometimes worry about whether they've arrived at a *sound* wish. They may feel a sense of uncertainty, from either a spiritual or ethical perspective, that a wish for personal attainment or achievement seems selfish or blindly materialistic. I was touched by the movie *Birdman* starring Michael Keaton, which has a surprising perspective on this question. Seen from a certain point of view, the hero, played by Keaton, is a self-centered, slightly over-the-hill movie star who is struggling to regain past glory.

But in the end, the film flips that conventional premise on its head. In fact, the protagonist comes to seem like a fairly decent, sincere man who is in his natural element in the spotlight. It is right and worthy for him to be on stage—whereas those who criticize him appear less and less compelling.

The movie asks you to take a careful inventory of your values, and to be certain that your ideas of right and wrong are authentic, and not just handed-down moralisms.

Similar to Keaton's antagonists in the movie, critics of self-help and motivational philosophy (sometimes taking aim at *The Secret*) argue that positive-mind principles and aspirational spirituality promote selfishness and self-centeredness. I question that.

Having been in this field a long time, I've never once seen anyone trying to manifest a Mercedes Benz (I never know where critics get that), or other objects of fleeting interest. Rather, I encounter people dealing with addictions, marital problems, career issues, illness, trouble paying the rent—things that are as real as life gets. But if someone *did* seek to manifest a shiny new car, or, more likely, some larger and more sustaining tangible achievement—as Keaton in the movie seeks renewed fame—I would defend that person. Who am I, or another, to judge what is natural, productive, and valuable in your life? I can easily imagine someone growing up in squalor, and simply wanting to experience beautiful objects and surroundings. That may not be *all* he wants, but it may represent something personally meaningful. Hence, his goal may involve the securing of material resources, perhaps through a particular line of business or profession.

Like all of us, Keaton's character in *Birdman* has a natural sense of what he needs to reach his highest potential. Neither he, nor anyone, should be made to feel shallow, or somehow "unspiritual," when longing to experience some form of material gain or individual achievement, of whatever nature. Wishes are complex and deeply intimate. Always aim for what truly matters to you. And never be too certain that the only things that matter are those we can't see. What counts most when devising a goal is your own highest sense of ethical attainment, personal excellence, and self-possession.

That is the raw material to bring to the Master Mind.

How the Master Mind Protects You

As we've been considering, the intentions of other people around you play a vital role in how your plans and ideas unfold. For this reason, Hill shared Roy Jarrett's principle that you should never casually disclose your ideas, dreams, and needs to just anyone. Hill especially cautioned against spilling plans in which you are deeply invested to random acquaintances, relatives, friends, and coworkers, who, through blithely (or even maliciously) tossed off opinions and judgments can shake your confidence, and contradict your best instincts and research.

"Without doubt, the most common weakness of all human beings," Hill wrote in *Think and Grow Rich*, "is the habit of leaving their minds open to the negative influence of other people. This weakness is all the more damaging, because most people do not recognize they are cursed by it, and many who acknowledge it, neglect or refuse to correct the evil until it becomes an uncontrollable part of their daily habits."

The only people with whom you should speak about your plans are those who possess specialized knowledge of your field, and the willingness to share or fairly sell that knowledge. The exception to this is your Master Mind alliance. This is a key benefit of working with a Master Mind group. The Master Mind group shields you from misdirected or ignorant remarks or opinions. This is a point that Hill repeatedly emphasized, and which bears returning to. He noted in *Think and Grow Rich*:

> Opinions are the cheapest commodities on earth. Everyone has a flock of opinions ready to

be wished upon anyone who will accept them. If you are influenced by "opinions" when you reach DECISIONS, you will not succeed in any undertaking, much less in that of transmuting YOUR OWN DESIRE into money.

If you are influenced by the opinions of others, you will have no DESIRE of your own.

Keep your own counsel, when you begin to put into practice the principles described here, by reaching your own decisions and following them.

Take no one into your confidence, EXCEPT the members of your "Master Mind" group, and be very sure in your selection of this group, that you choose ONLY those who will be in COMPLETE SYMPATHY AND HARMONY WITH YOUR PURPOSE.

As you can see from this quote, Hill's caution does not translate into adopting an attitude of caginess or cultivating isolation. Rather, the Master Mind becomes your intimate polity of friends, confidants, and peer advisers. You should see the group, both during meetings and off-times, as a roundtable, and each member as someone to whom you can divulge anything. You will, naturally, find many instances where you also need specialized advice, data, education, insight, and information from outside of your group. When such cases arise, as they inevitably will, consult with your Master Mind members about potential people and venues, consider the nature and quality of your sources, and seek out verifiably accurate information and legitimate experts. Be sure that you are receiving information from reputable sources. Again, never just someone with "opinions," which are a thinly veiled form of non-information.

As I alluded above, there is a psychological dimension to this caution. It is a hard truth of life that random people around you, including neighbors, coworkers, relatives, and even friends, can be jealous, covetous, or may derive a perverse thrill from denigrating other people's plans, dreams, and wishes. Such behavior is intended to salve their own regrets over unrealized ideas and ambitions. You will find these traits, sadly, in most of your social circles. Few people act on their ambitions, yet demonstrate no compunction about judging those of others. The Master Mind, and your own sense of discretion in selecting your sources, is a firewall against this kind of superfluous and potentially destructive communication.

Who Believes In You?

It is vital to be surrounded by the right kind of people— those who possess critical judgment, and believe in your abilities and aims. In his classic book *The Effective Executive*, published in 1966, management guru Peter Drucker—a brilliant and original thinker—promulgated three basic ideas to success, which have relevance to what we're studying. They are:

1. Build on islands of strength and health.

2. Work only on things that will make a great deal of difference if you succeed.

3. Work only with people who believe in what you're trying to accomplish.

Although item three was written just four years before Napoleon Hill's death, it could have come from his own pen, and it figures intimately into what we've been exploring. It may not always be possible to find yourself in the company of coworkers, backers, and collaborators who believe in what you're attempting. But the Master Mind, properly devised, will *always* believe in you, and lend surrogate support. It is both a practical and a moralizing force.

But it will remain so only through intra-group harmony. This is one more reason why you must never allow your Master Mind to sink into gossiping or opinion venting. Even outside of scheduled meetings, members should take care to avoid these practices. Take this opportunity to revisit the "no-gossip" pledge in chapter one. Reread it now.

On a visit to Bangladesh in 2017, Pope Francis called gossip "a kind of terrorism," and named it one of the "deadliest and most common" forms of social disintegration. "How many religious communities have been destroyed because of a spirit of gossip?" he asked. The same holds true of any fellowship. The further you keep frivolous or destructive modes of communication out of your Master Mind group, the greater it will serve you.

We've explored a wide range of group dynamics in this chapter. Napoleon Hill, in a sense, pioneered one of the most powerful and widespread self-help tools of the twentieth century and our own time: the support group.

His theory of the Master Mind, initially articulated in 1928, predated the 1935 formation of Alcoholics Anonymous, which helped popularize the concept of the "twelve steps" and the "group meeting." (The latter was also in practice as early as the 1910s by spiritual philosopher G.I. Gurdjieff.)

Although the aim of Alcoholics Anonymous is singular—to maintain sobriety—the overall twelve-step movement that grew from it addresses all kinds of life needs. The problems and aspirations that an individual can bring into the Master Mind are likewise boundless.

There is a link in the dynamics and makeup of the Master Mind and support-group models. Members of one group can learn from the experiences found in the other. Indeed, two of the four regulars of my Master Mind group are active twelve-steppers. The movements share key values: faith, persistence, and dedication to mutual aid. We now explore the complementary insights of each.

5

The Power of Peer Support

I once told a philosopher friend that it seemed to me that the age of great teachers had passed. The late-nineteenth and early-twentieth centuries, I said, saw a wave of innovative, iconic, and, in certain cases, extraordinarily important spiritual teachers—from the unclassifiable sage Jiddu Krishnamurti to the immensely important spiritual philosopher GI Gurdjieff to the Christian mystic and channeler Edgar Cayce. Yet our own era, while filled with colorful and infectious personalities, seems to lack teachers of real gravity and posterity. In chasing down social media followers, posting click-bait articles, and "branding" themselves, many of today's self-styled gurus convey a certain ordinariness.

"Why," I asked my friend, "don't we have great teachers today?"

"Today," he replied, "we have the group."

By "group" he meant a special and specific type of gathering. I think he would agree that several significant kinds of groups exist across our culture today. One of the most important is the recovery group, born out of the twelve-step tradition. Everything that I have written about the qualities of a Master Mind group applies to the recovery group. If you are in a recovery group, such as Alcoholics Anonymous, you are, in effect, already experiencing the benefits and potencies of a Master Mind fellowship, at least in one area of your life: the pursuit of sobriety. But the twelve-steps can be used for any number of life issues from gambling to debt-spending to overeating, and since the recovery-group model is so vital and prevalent within our culture, and it conveys and contains many of the qualities of a Master Mind group, I want to briefly turn attention to the origins and workings of the recovery group. My hope is that this chapter, and this book, will deepen both the Master Mind and support-group experience, and show how they relate to each other.

Let me note that a recovery group should not be seen as a substitute for the Master Mind, or vice versa. Each has its distinct purpose and reason for being. But, rather, the twelve steps are a sister movement and, for some people (including in my own group), an adjunct. Our understanding of one group can broaden and facilitate our participation in the other.

Recovery and the Master Mind

Along with Napoleon Hill, probably no other twentieth-century figures were more consequential in shaping the culture of self-help and mutual aid than Bill Wilson and Bob Smith, cofounders of Alcoholics Anonymous.

The Vermont-born men met in May 1935 in Akron, Ohio. Bill was a newly sober alcoholic travelling on business from New York. Alone at a hotel, he was desperate for a drink. He picked through a local church directory looking for a minister who could help him find another drunk to talk to. Bill had the idea that if he could locate another alcoholic to speak with, and to help, it might ease his own pangs for drink.

On that day, Bill found his way to Bob Smith, a local physician who had waged a long and losing battle with alcohol. Each man had spent years vainly trying out different ideas and treatments. When they met in Akron, however, each discovered that his inner resolve to stop drinking grew in proportion to his ability to counsel the other. Wilson and Smith's friendship resulted in the founding of Alcoholics Anonymous and the modern twelve-step fellowship.

Bill Wilson and Bob Smith appeared as all-American as their names. In their looks, dress, and politics, both men were as conservative as an old-fashioned banker, which Wilson actually was. But each man was also a spiritual adventurer, committed to traversing the terrain of metaphysical experience, from New Thought to Eastern metaphysics in search of a workable solution to addiction. Together, they wove Christian, Swedenborgian*, Jungian, Christian Science, and New Thought themes into the twelve steps of Alcoholics Anonymous.

---

* This is the philosophy of eighteenth-century mystic Emanuel Swedenborg, who is explored in "Appendix I: The Over-Soul: Inner Key to the Master Mind."

Though initially designed for alcoholism, the AA approach gave birth to the overall modern recovery movement. Its twelve-step model was later used to treat problems encompassing drug addiction, compulsive gambling, weight control, excessive spending, and chronic anger. AA altered the language of American life, giving rise to expressions such as "easy does it," "one day at a time," "first things first," and "let go and let God." Its literature also popularized an ecumenical term for the sacred: "Higher Power." (For Hill, of course, it was Master Mind or Infinite Intelligence.) This phrase appeared in the group's key principle that the alcoholic's "defense must come from a Higher Power," as Bill Wilson wrote in 1939. But Wilson and Smith insisted that twelve-steppers must form *their own* conception of God "*as we understood Him*," as the third step went. "Higher Power" neatly captured the radical ecumenism they were after.

Bill codified his spiritual experience into the first three steps of the twelve-step program. The first three steps were a kind of blueprint for an awakening or conversion experience. They were written in such a way that the word *alcohol* could be replaced by any other compulsory fixation, such as anger, drugs, or spending:

1. We admitted we were powerless over alcohol—that our lives had become unmanageable.

2. Came to believe that a Power greater than ourselves could restore us to sanity.

3. Made a decision to turn our will and our lives over to the care and direction of God *as we understood Him*.

Working as the chief writer, Bill published the twelve steps in 1939 in what became known as the "Big Book," *Alcoholics Anonymous*. While William James's work was central to Bill, many other influences shaped his outlook, including the teachings of the Oxford Group, an evangelical fellowship dedicated to mutual aid. One of the Oxford Group's key principles was that the sensitive, searching mind could bring a person to an experience of a Higher Power. This, in a sense, is also the underlying aim of the Master Mind: to access and apply higher energies of the mind, intuition, and perspective through an experience of Infinite Intelligence.

To facilitate its program, the Oxford Group pioneered the use of group meetings or "house parties." These took place in an encounter-group atmosphere of confession, meditation, shared testimonies, and joint prayer. Mutual help and lay therapy were central to Oxford's program, and gave rise to a similar structure in AA.* This, too, is indirectly reflected in the Master Mind.

Higher Versus Lower

One of the signature events of Bill Wilson's life came in the form of correspondence he had with Carl Jung in January 1961, in the last months of the psychologist's life. Bill wanted to tell Jung how his ideas had also impacted early twelve-steppers. To Bill's delight, the psychologist responded with a long and admiring letter on January 30. Jung repeated to Bill his formula for overcoming alco-

---

* There were also serious controversies around the Oxford Group's internal culture and leadership, which I consider in my book *One Simple Idea: How Positive Thinking Reshaped Modern Life*.

holism: *spiritus contra spiritum*. The Latin phrase could be roughly translated as: *Higher Spirit over lower spirits*, or alcohol. It was the twelve steps in a nutshell. This same "Higher Spirit," or Infinite Intelligence, is what Napoleon Hill hoped to tap through the Master Mind. Hill regarded thought, and particularly the subconscious, as a medium between man and higher energies.

As I've noted, it is unnecessary to see the Master Mind as a spiritual group—for many people it is not. But in the same way that Bill Wilson and his collaborators understood the group meeting as dispensing an additional, and sometimes ineffable, form of energy and insight to the efforts of its members, so did Hill see this dynamic at work in the Master Mind.

Although Hill's program is geared toward individual achievement, Hill also cautioned against a "go it alone" approach, which is, in many ways, the point of this book. To quote him again on the subject: "No individual may have great power without availing himself of the 'Master Mind.'"

Hill continued: "If you carry out these instructions with PERSISTENCE and intelligence, and use discrimination in the selection of your 'Master Mind' group, your objective will have been half-way reached, even before you begin to recognize it."

When referring to the "psychic phase" of the Master Mind, Hill wrote in terms that could have equally come from Bill Wilson: "The human mind is a form of energy, a part of it being spiritual in nature. When the minds of two people are coordinated in a SPIRIT OF HARMONY, the spiritual units of energy of each mind form an affinity . . ."

Again, Hill was not insistent on any spiritual or religious view—far from it. As a teacher, he, like Bill Wilson, was radically indifferent to one's personal spiritual outlook. If you find metaphysical language off-putting, you can just as easily—and validly—view this process of the pooling of intellects, or the emergence of a "third mind," as a metaphor; consider it a widely acknowledged outcome of the collaborative process that results from the efforts of a harmonious group, which heightens the insights and creative acumen of all its members. (Hill also used the metaphor of "thought energy" to compare a group of cooperative minds to conjoined electrical batteries.) In this vein, picture the mission control room at NASA (for a wonderful dramatization see the movie *Apollo 13*), the legendary garage where Steve Jobs and Steve Wozniak founded Apple, or the signers of the Declaration Hill described in the previous chapter.

All of this spells out why the support-group element of Hill's program—so easy to neglect in a our digital age where we focus individually on screens and devices—remains as critical in the twenty-first century as when Hill first articulated the idea in the 1920s.

ACTION STEP:
Your Master Mind Cards

The strength of the twelve-step, Master Mind, and mutual-support model can reach you through unexpected channels. For my mother-in-law, Terri Orr, a retired Harvard Medical School dean and a woman of extraordinary accomplishment, a special source of power and personal help arrived through her lifelong habit of writing small reminders to affirmative faith, which was part of her own twelve-step activities. In effect, the writing and sharing of affirmations became Terri's method of passing on the power of the Master Mind.

This practice was the first thing I noticed more than twenty years ago when she and I met. The rooms of Terri's cramped two-family home in Waltham, Massachusetts, where she singlehandedly raised two daughters and looked after an elderly mother, were papered—on the refrigerator, medicine chest, above the kitchen sink, on mirrors and closet doors—with business-sized cards on which she wrote daily affirming quotes, mottoes, twelve-step principles, and Scriptural passages, such as:

> "Being too serious about all I have to do
> can make me unrealistic."

> "When am I going to stop going to
> the hardware store for milk?"

> "If anyone speaks badly of you,
> live so that none will believe it."

> "It's not my life, it's just my lunch."

One of Terri's favorite cards—"waiting has more power than an ill-timed decision"—proved a helpful piece of counsel to a Harvard Medical

School student. One day, she was talking with the student at a coffee machine. He confided to her that he was having problems with his girlfriend—he was unsure about their future, and whether to push for a commitment. As a financial aid administrator, Terri often heard about students' personal lives. "When you talk money with a student," she observed, "you get into very intimate family details. So, I knew my students pretty well.

"And I was able to say to him: *'Waiting has more power than an ill-timed decision'*—and his eyes opened wide. I don't know what the outcome was; but at that moment it seemed like something that had been useful to him, as it had been to me," she said.

"I often found that there might be a message from the cards that I could pass on to others." This was the Master Mind principle in action.

Write down at least three personal aphorisms that you would like to share with your Master Mind group. Bring them into your next meeting, and ask others to do the same. You can set aside time at the end where everyone reads his or her aphorisms. Here are some samples that have been quoted in my own meetings:

"A full bag is heavy, but an empty
bag is heavier." (Jewish proverb)

"Perfect is good, done is better." (Terri Orr)

"Keep punching." (Lou Murray)

"The infallible index of true progress
is found in the tone the man takes."
(Emerson, "The Over-Soul")

"The fear disappears once you
step right into it."

"God speaks in principles, not occurrences."

What are your aphorisms to live by?

6

Think and Grow Rich: A Master Mind Way of Life

As I noted earlier, *Think and Grow Rich* is the foundation for many of the ideas in this book. Hill's 1937 work is vital reading. It has probably touched more people than any other work of modern self-help. I have met artists, business people, doctors, teachers, athletes—people from different professions and possessed of seemingly different outer goals—who have attested that *Think and Grow Rich* made a decisive difference in their lives.

Try a small personal experiment: visibly carry a copy of *Think and Grow Rich* with you through an airport, grocery store, shopping mall, or any public place—and see if more than one person doesn't stop you and say something like, "Now, *that's* a great book . . ." If you do this more than once, you'll be struck by the diversity of people who approach you.

Think and Grow Rich has sold many millions of copies around the world since its first appearance—but that is not the true measure of its success. Lots of books gain popularity for a time, but go unread, and sometimes unheard of, within a decade or so of their publication. But *Think and Grow Rich* has, if anything, grown in influence since Hill's death in 1970. Its ideas are at the foundation of most of today's philosophies of business motivation and personal achievement. More so, the book has given people a sense of their own veritable possibilities. It has provided readers with that rarest of gifts: realistic self-belief. It is a philosophy that uplifts the individual.

For these reasons, I am providing this chapter as a reliable digest of *Think and Grow Rich*, which can be used as a refresher by you and your Master Mind colleagues. It is not a substitute for the original, but it is a sturdy primer and reminder of the principles of this seminal work. Turn to it whenever you have questions on your Master Mind journey, or feel uncertain of your path.

As you read, or reread, these thirteen steps, always hold in mind how you can bring them in front of your Master Mind group for expansion and application. The Master Mind is the binding agent that holds together and amplifies your plans—indeed, you will see that several of these steps reference the Master Mind. Your group members will help you see and execute these steps from unexpected angles, and find new possibilities within them.

If you come across steps that you've previously neglected—or that need freshening (and we all have them)—write them down as special items to take up with your Master Mind partners. Here is Hill's advice from *Think and Grow Rich*, with his emphasis in the original:

> Every plan you adopt, in your endeavor to accumulate wealth, should be the joint creation of yourself and every other member of your "Master Mind" group. You may originate your own plans, either in whole or in part, but SEE THAT THOSE PLANS ARE CHECKED, AND APPOVED THE BY MEMBERS OF YOUR "MASTER MIND" ALLIANCE.

This condensation mostly retains Hill's original terms, stylistic choices, capitalizations, and emphases to preserve, as closely as possible, his manner of expression and priorities.

Desire: *The First Step to Riches*

In the early twentieth century a great American salesman and businessman named Edwin C. Barnes discovered how we truly *think and grow rich*.

Barnes's discovery did not come in one sitting. It came little by little, beginning with an ALL-CONSUMING DESIRE to become a business associate of inventor Thomas Edison. One of the chief characteristics of Barnes's desire was that it was *definite*. Barnes wanted to work *with* Edison—not just *for* him.

Straight off a freight train, Barnes presented himself in 1905 at Edison's New Jersey laboratory. He announced that he had come to go into business with the inventor. In speaking of their meeting years later,

Edison said: "He stood there before me, looking like an ordinary tramp, but there was something in the expression of his face which conveyed the impression that he was determined to get what he had come after."

Barnes did *not* get his partnership with Edison on his first interview. But he *did* get a chance to work in the Edison offices, at a very nominal wage, doing a job that was unimportant to Edison—but very *important* to Barnes, because it gave him an opportunity to display his abilities to his future "partner."

Months passed. Nothing happened outwardly to bring Barnes any closer to his goal. But something important *was* happening in Barnes's mind. He was constantly intensifying his CHIEF DESIRE and his PLANS to become Edison's business associate.

Barnes was DETERMINED TO REMAIN READY UNTIL HE GOT THE OPPORTUNITY HE CAME FOR.

When the "big chance" arrived, it was in a different form, and from a different direction, than Barnes had expected. *That is one of the tricks of opportunity.* It has a sly habit of slipping in by the back door, and it often comes disguised as misfortune or temporary defeat. Perhaps this is why so many fail to wait for—or recognize—opportunity when it arrives.

Edison had just perfected a new device, known then as the Edison Dictating Machine. His salesmen were unenthused. But Barnes saw his opportunity hidden in a strange-looking contraption that interested no one. Barnes seized the chance to sell the dictating machine, and did it so successfully that Edison gave him a contract to distribute and market it all over the world.

When Edwin C. Barnes climbed down from that freight train in Orange, New Jersey, he possessed one CONSUMING OBSESSION: to become the business associate of the great inventor. Barnes's desire was not a *hope!* It was not a *wish!* It was a keen, pulsating DESIRE, which transcended everything else. It was DEFINITE.

Wishing will not bring riches or other forms of success. But *desiring* riches with a state of mind that becomes an obsession, then planning definite ways and means to acquire riches, and backing those plans with persistence *that does not recognize failure*, will bring success.

The method by which DESIRE can be transmuted into its financial equivalent, consists of six definite, practical steps.

First. Fix in your mind the *exact* amount of money you desire. It is not sufficient merely to say, "I want plenty of money." Be definite as to the amount.

Second. Determine exactly what you intend to give in return for the money you desire.

Third. Establish a definite date when you intend to *possess* the money you desire.

Fourth. Create *a definite plan* for carrying out your desire, and begin *at once*, whether or not you are ready, to put this plan into *action*.

Fifth. Write out a clear, concise statement of the amount of money you intend to acquire, name the time limit for its acquisition, state what you intend to give in return for the money, and describe clearly the plan through which you intend to accumulate it.

Sixth. Read your written statement aloud, twice daily, once just before retiring at night and once after arising in the morning. AS YOU READ—SEE AND FEEL AND BELIEVE YOURSELF ALREADY IN POSSESSION OF THE MONEY.

It is especially important that you observe and follow number six. You may complain that it is impossible for you to "see yourself in possession of money" before you actually have it. Here is where a BURNING DESIRE will come to your aid. If you truly DESIRE money or another goal so keenly that your desire is an obsession, you will have no difficulty in convincing yourself that you will acquire it. The object is to want it so much and become so determined that you CONVINCE yourself you will have it.

Faith: *The Second Step to Riches*

FAITH is the head chemist of the mind. When FAITH is blended with the vibration of thought, the subconscious mind instantly picks up the vibration, translates it into its spiritual equivalent, and transmits it to Infinite Intelligence, as in the case of prayer.

ALL THOUGHTS THAT HAVE BEEN EMO-TIONALIZED (given feeling) AND MIXED WITH FAITH begin immediately to translate themselves into their physical equivalent.

If you have difficulty getting a grasp of just what faith is, think of it as a special form of *persistence*—one that we feel when we *know* that we have right at our backs and that helps us persevere through setbacks and temporary failure.

To develop this quality in yourself, use this five-step formula. Promise yourself to read, repeat, and abide by these steps—and write down your promise.

First. I know that I have the ability to achieve the object of my DEFINITE PURPOSE in life, therefore, I *demand* of myself persistent, continuous action toward its attainment, and I here and now promise to render such action.

Second. I realize the dominating thoughts of my mind will eventually reproduce themselves in outward physical action, and gradually transform themselves into physical reality. Therefore, I will concentrate my thoughts for thirty minutes daily upon the task of thinking of the person I intend to become, thereby creating in my mind a clear mental picture of that person.

Third. I know that through the principle of autosuggestion (i.e., the suggestions we make to ourselves—see step three) any desire that I persistently hold in my mind will eventually seek expression through some practical means of attaining the object back of it. Therefore, I will devote ten minutes daily to demanding of myself the development of *self-confidence*.

Fourth. I have clearly written down a description of my DEFINITE CHIEF AIM in life, and I will never stop trying until I have developed sufficient self-confidence for its attainment.

Fifth. I fully realize that no wealth or position can long endure unless built upon truth and justice. Therefore, I will engage in no transaction that does not benefit all whom it affects. I will succeed by attracting to myself the forces I wish to use, and the cooperation of other people. I will induce others to serve me, because of my willingness to serve others. I will eliminate hatred, envy, jealousy, selfishness, and cynicism, by developing love for all humanity, because I know that a negative attitude toward others can never bring me success. I will cause others to believe in me because I will believe in them, and in myself.

I will sign my name to this formula, commit it to memory, and repeat it aloud once a day, with full FAITH that it will gradually influence my THOUGHTS and ACTIONS, so that I will become a self-reliant and successful person.

Autosuggestion: *The Third Step to Riches*

AUTOSUGGESTION is a term that applies to all suggestions and self-administered stimuli that reach one's mind through the five senses. Stated another way: *autosuggestion is self-suggestion.*

It is the agency of communication between the conscious and subconscious minds. But your subconscious mind recognizes and acts ONLY upon thoughts that have been well mixed with *emotion or feeling.* This is a fact of such importance as to warrant repetition.

When you begin to use—and keep using—the three-step program for autosuggestion in this segment, be on the alert for hunches from your subconscious mind—and when they appear, put them into ACTION IMMEDIATELY.

First. Go into some quiet spot (preferably in bed at night) where you will not be disturbed or interrupted, close your eyes, and repeat aloud (so you may hear your own words) the written statement of the amount of money you intend to accumulate, the time limit for its accumulation, and a description of the service or merchandise you intend to give in return for the money. As you carry out these instructions SEE YOURSELF ALREADY IN POSSESSION OF THE MONEY.

For example: Suppose that you intend to accumulate $50,000 by the first of January, five years hence, and that you intend to give personal services in return for the money in the capacity of a salesman. Your written statement of your purpose should be similar to the following:

"By the first day of January, I will have in my possession $50,000, which will come to me in various amounts from time to time during the interim.

"In return for this money I will give the most efficient service of which I am capable, rendering the fullest possible quantity and the best possible quality of service in the capacity of salesman of _____ (and describe the service or merchandise you intend to sell).

"I believe that I will have this money in my possession. My faith is so strong that I can now see this money before my eyes. I can touch it with my hands. It is now awaiting transfer to me at the time and in the proportion that I deliver the service I intend to render for it. I am awaiting a plan by which to accumulate this money, and I will follow that plan when it is received."

Second. Repeat this program night and morning until you can see (in your imagination) the money you intend to accumulate.

Third. Place a written copy of your statement where you can see it night and morning, and read it just before retiring and upon arising, until it has been memorized.

Specialized Knowledge:
The Fourth Step to Riches

General knowledge, no matter how great in quantity or variety, is of little use in accumulating money. Knowledge is only *potential* power. It becomes power only when, and if, it is organized into *definite plans of action*, and directed toward a *definite end*.

In connection with your aim, you must decide what sort of specialized knowledge you require, and the purpose for which it is needed. To a large extent, your major purpose in life, and the goal toward which you are working, will help determine what knowledge you need. With this question settled, your next move requires that you have ACCURATE INFORMATION concerning DEPENDABLE SOURCES OF KNOWLEDGE.

Look toward many high-quality sources for the knowledge you seek: people, courses, partnerships, books—look everywhere. Some of this knowledge will be free—never undervalue what is free—and some will require purchasing. Decide what knowledge you seek—and pursue it completely. The author spent more than twenty years interviewing people and studying success methods before writing *Think and Grow Rich.*

Without specialized knowledge, your ideas remain mere wishes. Once you have acquired the knowledge you need, you can use your critical faculty of *imagination* to combine your IDEAS with this SPECIALIZED KNOWLEDGE, and make ORGANIZED PLANS to carry out your aims.

This is the formula for capability: *Using imagination to combine specialized knowledge with ideas, and to form organized plans.*

The connecting ingredient is imagination, which we will now learn to cultivate.

Imagination: *The Fifth Step to Riches*

The imagination is the workshop wherein are fashioned all plans created by man. The impulse, the DESIRE, is literally given shape, form, and ACTION through the aid of the imaginative faculty of the mind.

Through the medium of creative imagination, the finite mind of man has direct communication with Infinite Intelligence. Imagination is the faculty through which "hunches" and "inspirations" are reached. It is by this faculty that all basic or new ideas are handed over to man. It is through this faculty that thought vibrations from the minds of others are received. It is through this faculty that one individual may "tune in" or communicate with the subconscious minds of others.

The creative imagination works only when the conscious mind is stimulated through the emotion of a STRONG DESIRE. This is highly significant.

What's more, the creative faculty may have become weak through inaction. Your imagination becomes more alert and more receptive in proportion to its development through *use*.

After you have completed this book, return to this section and begin at once to put your imagination to work on the building of a plan, or plans, for the transmutation of *desire* into money, or your core aim. Reduce your plan to writing. The moment you complete this, you will have *definitely* given concrete form to the intangible *desire*.

This step is extremely important. When you reduce the statement of your desire and a plan for its realization, into writing, you have actually *taken the first* of a series of steps that will enable you to covert your *thought* into its physical counterpart.

Organized Planning: *The Sixth Step to Riches*

It is vital that you form a DEFINITE, practical plan, or plans, to carry out your aims. You will now learn how to build plans that are *practical*, as follows:

First. Ally yourself with a group of as many people as you may need for the creation and carrying out of your plan or plans for the accumulation of money—making use of the Master Mind principle. (As noted, compliance with this instruction is essential. Do not neglect it.)

Second. Before forming your Master Mind alliance, decide what advantages and benefits you may offer the individual members of your group in return for their cooperation. As explored, no one will work indefinitely without some form of compensation. No intelligent person will either request or expect another to work without adequate compensation, although this may not always be in the form of money.

Third. Arrange to meet with the members of your Master Mind group at least twice a week,* and more often if possible, until you have jointly perfected the necessary plan or plans for the accumulation of money.

Fourth. Maintain *perfect harmony* between yourself and every member of your Master Mind group. If you fail to carry out this instruction to the letter, you may expect to meet with failure. The Master Mind principle *cannot* obtain where *perfect harmony* does not prevail.

Keep in mind these facts:

1. You are engaged in an undertaking of major importance to you. To be sure of success, you must have plans that are faultless.

2. You must have the advantage of the experience, education, native ability, and imagination of other minds. This is in harmony with the methods

---

* I have modified Hill's original instruction to once a week, which I think is more practical in today's environment. If circumstances permit, you can certainly meet more than once a week.

followed by every person who has accumulated a great fortune.

Now, if the first plan you devise does not work successfully, replace it with a new plan. If this new plan fails to work, replace it, in turn, with still another, and so on, until you find a plan that *does work*. Right here is the point where the majority of men meet with failure, because of their lack of *persistence* in creating new plans to take the place of those that fail.

Remember this when your plans fail: *Temporary defeat is not permanent failure.*

No follower of this philosophy can reasonably expect to accumulate a fortune without experiencing "temporary defeat." When defeat comes, accept it as a signal that your plans are not sound, rebuild those plans, and set sail once more toward your goal.

Finally, as you are devising your plans keep in mind these Major Attributes of Leadership – traits possessed by the greatest achievers:

1. Unwavering Courage

2. Self-Control

3. A Keen Sense of Justice

4. Definiteness of Decision

5. Definiteness of Plans

6. The Habit of Doing More Than Paid For

7.   A Pleasing Personality

8.   Sympathy and Understanding

9.   Mastery of Detail

10.   Willingness to Assume Full Responsibility

11.   Cooperation With Others

Decision: *The Seventh Step to Riches*

Analysis of several hundred people who had accumulated fortunes disclosed that *every one of them* had the habit of *reaching decisions promptly,* and of changing these decisions slowly, if and when they were changed. People who fail to accumulate money, *without exception,* have the habit of reaching decisions, if at all, very *slowly,* and of *changing these decisions quickly and often.*

What's more, the majority of people who fail to accumulate money sufficient for their needs tend to be easily influenced by the "opinions" of others. As noted, "opinions" are the cheapest commodities on earth. Everyone has a flock of opinions ready to be wished upon anyone who will accept them. If you are influenced by "opinions" when you reach *decisions,* you will not succeed in any undertaking, much less in that of transmuting *your own desire* into money.

If you are influenced by the opinions of others, you will have no DESIRE of your own.

Keep your own counsel when you begin to put into practice the principles described here by *reaching your own decisions* and following them. Take no one into your confidence *except* the members of your Master Mind group, and be very sure in your selection of this group that you choose ONLY those who will be in COMPLETE SYMPATHY AND HARMONY WITH YOUR PURPOSE.

Close friends and relatives, while not meaning to, often handicap one through "opinions" and sometimes through ridicule, which is meant to be humorous. Thousands of men and women carry inferiority complexes with them throughout life, because some well-meaning but ignorant person destroyed their confidence through "opinions" or ridicule.

You have a mind of your own. USE IT and reach your own decisions. If you need facts or information from others to enable you to reach decisions, as you probably will in many instances, acquire these facts or secure the information you need quietly, without disclosing your purpose.

Those who reach DECISIONS promptly and definitely know what they want and generally get it. Leaders in every walk of life DECIDE quickly and firmly. That is the major reason why they are leaders. The world has a habit of making room for the man whose words and actions show that he knows where he is going.

Persistence: *The Eighth Step to Riches*
PERSISTENCE is an essential factor in transmuting DESIRE into its monetary equivalent. The basis of persistence is the POWER OF WILL.

Willpower and desire, when properly combined,

make an irresistible pair. Men who accumulate great fortunes are generally known as cold-blooded and sometimes ruthless. Often they are misunderstood. What they have is willpower, which they mix with persistence, and place at the back of their desires to *ensure* the attainment of their objectives.

Lack of persistence is one of the major causes of failure. Experience with thousands of people has proved that lack of persistence is a weakness common to the majority of men. It is a weakness that may be overcome by effort. The ease with which lack of persistence may be conquered depends *entirely* upon the INTENSITY OF ONE'S DESIRE.

In short, THERE IS NO SUBSTITUTE FOR PERSISTENCE! It cannot be supplanted by any other quality! Remember this and it will hearten you in the beginning when the going may seem difficult and slow.

Those who have cultivated the HABIT of persistence seem to enjoy insurance against failure. No matter how many times they are defeated, they finally arrive toward the top of the ladder. Sometimes it appears that there is a hidden Guide whose duty is to test men through all sorts of discouraging experiences. Those who pick themselves up after defeat and keep on trying arrive at their destination. The hidden Guide lets no one enjoy great achievement without passing the PERSISTENCE TEST.

What we DO NOT SEE, what most of us never suspect of existing, is the silent but irresistible POWER that comes to the rescue of those who fight on in the face of discouragement. If we speak of this power at all, we call it PERSISTENCE.

There are four simple steps that lead to the habit of PERSISTENCE.

1. A definite purpose backed by burning desire for its fulfillment.

2. A definite plan, expressed in continuous action.

3. A mind closed tightly against all negative and discouraging influences, including negative suggestions of relatives, friends, and acquaintances.

4. A friendly alliance with one or more persons who will encourage you to follow through with both plan and purpose.

The Master Mind: *The Ninth Step to Riches*

We now come to the center point of this book.

As noted earlier, the Master Mind may be defined as: "Coordination of knowledge and effort, in a spirit of harmony, between two or more people for the attainment of a definite purpose."

No individual may hold great power without availing himself of the Master Mind. The sixth step supplied instructions for the creation of PLANS for the purpose of translating DESIRE into its monetary equivalent. If you carry out these instructions with PERSISTENCE and intelligence, and use discrimination in selecting your Master Mind group, your objective will have been halfway reached, even before you begin to recognize it.

The Master Mind brings an obvious economic advantage, by allowing you to surround yourself with the advice, counsel, and personal cooperation of a group of people who are willing to lend you wholehearted aid in a spirit of PERFECT HARMONY. But there is also a more abstract phase; it may be called the PSYCHIC PHASE.*

The psychic phase of the Master Mind is more difficult to comprehend because it has reference to the spiritual forces with which the human race, as a whole, is not well acquainted. You may catch a significant suggestion from this statement: "No two minds ever come together without, thereby, creating a third invisible, intangible force which may be likened to a third mind."

The human mind is a form of energy, a part of it being spiritual in nature. When the minds of two people are coordinated in a SPIRIT OF HARMONY the spiritual units of energy of each mind form an affinity, which constitutes the "psychic" phase of the Master Mind.

Analyze the record of any man who has accumulated a great fortune, and many of those who have accumulated modest fortunes, and you will find that they have either consciously or unconsciously employed the Master Mind.

Great power can be accumulated through no other principle!

---

* I do not analyze the question of a "psychic" component to the Master Mind in this book. For more on that topic, see my book *The Miracle Club*.

Sex Transmutation: *The Tenth Step to Riches*

The meaning of the word "transmute" is, in simple language, "the changing or transferring of one element, or form of energy, into another." The emotion of sex brings into being a unique and powerful state of mind that can be used for extraordinary intellectual and material creative purposes.

This is accomplished through *sex transmutation*, which means the switching of the mind from thoughts of physical expression to thoughts of some other nature.

Sex is the most powerful of human desires. When driven by this desire, men develop keenness of imagination, courage, willpower, persistence, and creative ability unknown to them at other times. So strong and impelling is the desire for sexual contact that men freely run the risk of life and reputation to indulge it.

When harnessed and redirected along other lines, this motivating force maintains all of its attributes of keenness of imagination, courage, etc., which may be used as powerful creative forces in literature, art, or in any other profession or calling, including, of course, the accumulation of riches.

The transmutation of sex energy calls for the exercise of willpower, to be sure, but the reward is worth the effort. The desire for sexual expression is inborn and natural. The desire cannot, and should not, be submerged or eliminated. But it should be given an outlet through forms of expression that enrich the body, mind, and spirit. If not given this form of outlet, through transmutation, it will seek outlets through purely physical channels.

The emotion of sex is an "irresistible force." When driven by this emotion, men become gifted with a super power for action. Understand this truth, and you will catch the significance of the statement that sex transmutation will lift one into the status of a genius. The emotion of sex contains the secret of creative ability.

When harnessed and transmuted, this driving force is capable of lifting men to that higher sphere of thought which enables them to master the sources of worry and petty annoyance that beset their pathway on the lower plane.

The major reason why the majority of men who succeed do not begin to do so until after the ages of forty to fifty (or beyond), is their tendency to DISSIPATE their energies through over indulgence in physical expression of the emotion of sex. The majority of men *never* learn that the urge of sex has other possibilities, which far transcend in importance that of mere physical expression.

But remember, sexual energy must be *transmuted* from desire for physical contact into some *other* form of desire and action, in order to lift one to the status of a genius.

The Subconscious Mind:
The Eleventh Step to Riches

The subconscious mind is the connecting link between the finite mind of man and Infinite Intelligence. It is the intermediary through which one may draw upon the forces of Infinite Intelligence at will. It alone contains the secret process by which mental impulses are modified and changed into their spiritual equivalent. It alone is the medium through which prayer may be transmitted to the source capable of answering prayer.

It is difficult to approach the discussion of the subconscious mind without a feeling of littleness and inferiority due, perhaps, to the fact that man's entire stock of knowledge on the subject is so limited. The very fact that the subconscious mind is the medium of communication between the thinking mind of man and Infinite Intelligence is, of itself, a thought that almost paralyzes one's reason.

After you have accepted as a reality the existence of your subconscious mind, and understand its possibilities for transmuting your DESIRES into their physical or monetary equivalent, you will understand why you have been repeatedly urged to MAKE YOUR DESIRES CLEAR, AND TO REDUCE THEM TO WRITING. You will also understand the necessity of PERSISTENCE in carrying out instructions. The thirteen principles in this program are the stimuli with which—through practice and persistence—you acquire the ability to reach and influence your subconscious mind.

The Brain: *The Twelfth Step to Riches*

More than twenty years before writing *Think and Grow Rich*, the author, working with Dr. Alexander Graham Bell and Dr. Elmer R. Gates, observed that every human brain is both a broadcasting and receiving station for the vibration of thought.

The Creative Imagination is the "receiving set" of the brain, which receives thoughts released by the brains of others. It is the agency of communication between one's conscious, or reasoning, mind, and the outer sources from which one may receive thought stimuli.

When stimulated, or "stepped up," to a high rate of vibration, the mind becomes more receptive to the vibration of thought from outside sources. This "stepping up" occurs through the positive emotions or the negative emotions. Through the emotions the vibrations of thought may be increased. This is why it is crucial that your goal have strong emotions at the back of it.

Vibrations of an exceedingly high rate are the only vibrations picked up and carried from one brain to another. Thought is energy travelling at an exceedingly high rate of vibration. Thought that has been modified or "stepped up" by any of the major emotions vibrates at a much higher rate than ordinary thought, and it is this type of thought that passes from one mind to another, through the broadcasting machinery of the human brain.

Thus, you will see that the broadcasting principle is the factor through which you mix feeling or emotion with your thoughts and pass them on to your subconscious mind, or to the minds of others.

The Sixth Sense:
The Thirteenth Step to Riches
The thirteenth and final principle is known as the "sixth sense," through which Infinite Intelligence may and will communicate voluntarily, without any effort or demands by the individual.

After you have mastered the principles in this book, you will be prepared to accept as true a statement that may otherwise seem incredible: Through the aid of the sixth sense you will be warned of impending dangers in time to avoid them, and notified of opportunities in time to embrace them.

With the development of the sixth sense, there comes to your aid, and to do your bidding, a kind of "guardian angel" who will open to you at all times the door to the Temple of Wisdom.

Whether this is a statement of truth, you will never know except by following the instructions described in this program, or some similar method.

The author of *Think and Grow Rich* is not a believer in, nor an advocate of, "miracles," for the reason that he has enough knowledge of Nature to understand that Nature *never deviates from her established laws*. Some of her laws are so incomprehensible that they produce what appear to be "miracles." The sixth sense approaches this status.

A Final Word About Fear

As you begin any new undertaking you are likely at one point or another to find yourself gripped by the emotion of fear.

Fear should never be bargained with or capitulated to. It takes the charm from one's personality, destroys the possibility of accurate thinking, diverts concentration of effort, masters persistence, turns the willpower into nothingness, destroys ambition, beclouds the memory, and invites failure in every conceivable form. It kills love, assassinates the finer emotions of the heart, discourages friendship, and leads to sleeplessness, misery, and unhappiness.

So pernicious and destructive is the emotion of fear that it is, almost literally, worse than anything that can befall you.

If you suffer from a fear of poverty, reach a decision to get along with whatever wealth you can accumulate WITHOUT WORRY. If you fear the loss of love, reach a decision to get along without love, if that is necessary. If you experience a general sense of worry, reach a blanket decision that *nothing* life has to offer is *worth* the price of worry.

And remember: The greatest of all remedies for fear is a BURNING DESIRE FOR ACHIEVEMENT, backed by useful service to others.

7

Master Mind Questions and Answers

Now that you've studied the dynamics of the Master Mind, and have an understanding of its central role and function in Napoleon Hill's program, you are probably harboring questions about forming and maintaining your own alliance. This chapter addresses some of the most common questions about running your group. Nothing about this process should vex you, and this chapter helps put your concerns to rest.

Q: Who should I initially approach to start a group?
A: I recommend beginning with friends and coworkers who already have a demonstrated interest in self-help, and with whom you may have already discussed Napoleon Hill or related authors. You're not trying to convert anyone to anything. You want to start by reaching out to people who already possess an earnest interest in

self-help and motivational philosophy. Ensure that you are on the same page in terms of ideals. And—the all-important factor—that you have agreeable chemistry. Also, I wouldn't necessarily recommend approaching people with whom you're *too* close, such as a spouse. This is so you can bring a sense of fresh history to the project.

Q: Can we invite new members to an existing group?
A: Absolutely. If new members weren't welcome, I never would have joined my own Master Mind group. My group began in spring 2008, and I did not join until summer 2013. The key thing is to select new members who are in sync with the group's values, tone, and style. If your group tends to be religious in nature (like my own), you'll want people who are at ease with that, and can contribute to the group atmosphere. It is important to cultivate the growth and sustenance of your group on *its own terms*, as you would a garden or farm, adding things that are natural to its climate. The point is not to bring in newcomers to upend or change what you're doing, but rather to help your group continue to flourish. Comity and harmony are vital.

Q: Can I just join a group that's already formed?
A: Definitely. As noted, that's how I came into my group. The key thing—as with inviting members into an existing group, or recruiting people to start a new one—is finding the right fit. If you already have friends or colleagues in a Master Mind group, you can approach them about joining. And respect their

response. Sometimes people want to maintain the balance and intimacy of their current group. Other times they may be on the lookout for new members, and will be delighted to learn of your interest. I would not approach a stranger about joining his group. It is best to have an anchor in someone you already know and respect.

Q: We have a member who never or rarely shows—should we eject him?
A: I don't recommend it. It is all but inevitable that you will have members who drift away, pull no-shows, or seldom participate. My advice is: let them be. Do not seek confrontation or formal (or informal) expulsions. If the person swings back into participation, that's all to the good. If he or she drifts away, let the individual to go in peace. And even if someone seems to perpetually come and go—which is not ideal since it disassociates him from the flow and context of the group—I still counsel forbearance. Conflict stifles the Master Mind. One of the worst group decisions I ever witnessed was when a circle of people decided that two members weren't fitting in with the nature of a certain group. They attempted to diplomatically explain this to the pair and exclude them. The group members felt that they were just being honest, but feelings were profoundly hurt on all sides, and the whole group soon disbanded. The key thing is to ensure that you simply have enough steady members to keep your meeting flowing each week—the minimum is two. You can always add newcomers, which is a far better fix than expulsions.

Q: How should we handle it when a member strays from the topic, or whose comments often meander?

A: This is where you must be constructively assertive of the aims and structure of the group. It falls to each week's rotating leader to do this, though others can take the initiative, as well. It is vital that the group's structure and ground rules, as outlined in Chapter Two, be followed—although your group may, of course, adapt and reform some of these rules. Once a steady format is settled upon, it behooves each member—as a matter of respect for the group and its goals—to honor it, and to be structured, steady, and focused in comments and exchanges. One time in my group, a member who had been absent for a while returned to the call and a spent a fairly liberal amount of time catching up, and describing a personal project. At one point, another member interjected that this sundry conversation had been going on for about forty minutes, and he wanted the meeting to get underway at its usual pace. We quickly switched gears. His correction was entirely right and necessary. Everyone has his own pace and manner—and it's natural, for instance, that some members may be more talkative than others. But all are required to abide by a sense of format, focus, and reasonable expeditiousness.

Q: Our group is a mixture of spiritual and non-spiritual people. How do we deal with matters of prayer and meditation?

A: Broadly speaking, the Master Mind, and the book *Think and Grow Rich* have a spiritual component, which is to say that when writing about the Master Mind,

Hill described extra-physical factors and possibilities, such as tapping Infinite Intelligence. Hence, many Master Mind participants find it natural to use prayers, meditations, affirmations, visualizations, and various techniques from the positive-mind tradition, as well as from their own faiths. If spirituality matters to you, you may want to seek like-valued collaborators. That said, a Master Mind group can absolutely be conducted along non-spiritual lines. Goal-setting exercises and personal contracts, for example, involve holding yourself to your highest standards, and are not necessarily spiritual in nature. Affirmations and meditations can also serve ethical and psychological ends. Enough evidence exists within various branches of cognitive psychology to support the use of well-formulated affirmations, visualizations, and self-suggestion for purposes of conditioning, expanded thinking, and goal-setting. For a distinctly secular sounding of mind-power philosophy, I recommend reading Maxwell Maltz's 1960 book *Psycho-Cybernetics*. The author, a pioneering cosmetic surgeon, worked out an entire program of self-development based on meditation, visualization, and affirmation, without an element of spirituality. Spiritual and non-spiritual group members will find a great deal of common ground in Maltz's book.

Q: I've heard that Napoleon Hill never had a Master Mind group—but instead he conducted imaginary conservations with historical figures. Can't I just do that, too?

A: In *Think and Grow Rich*, Hill described regularly convening an "imaginary council" of historical eminences, from whom he received guidance, advice, and lessons in character building. But he never called that a substitute for a Master Mind group, for him or anyone. Recall the testimony of John Gilmore of the Open Heart Spiritual Center in Memphis from Chapter Two: John's Master Mind group used imaginary discussions with historical figures to augment—not substitute for—their meetings. Hill described his "imaginary council" technique this way in *Think and Grow Rich*, "Chapter Fourteen: The Sixth Sense:"

> Long before I had ever written a line for publication, or endeavored to deliver a speech in public, I followed the habit of reshaping my own character, by trying to imitate nine men whose lives and life-works had been most important to me. These nine men were, Emerson, Paine, Edison, Darwin, Lincoln, Burbank, Napoleon, Ford, and Carnegie. I held an imaginary Council meeting with this group whom I called my "Invisible Counselors."
>
> The procedure was this. Just before going to sleep at night, I would shut my eyes, and see in my imagination, this group of men seated with me around my Council Table. Here I had not only an opportunity to sit among those whom I considered to be great, but I actually dominated the group, by serving as the Chairman.

If this kind of practice appeals to you and your group members, you can try it individually, perhaps taking turns and reporting back results and insights to your group. The full procedure appears in *Think and Grow Rich*, and I quote one of Hill's imaginary dialogues in the following question. Remember: this practice is an augmentation to the Master Mind, but not a substitute.

Q: Break it down for me. What REALLY happens in the Master Mind, in physical, empirical terms?
A: I mentioned earlier that I wouldn't spend much of this book analyzing metaphysics. This is a book of application and practice. But there is an intriguing and overlooked passage toward the end of *Think and Grow Rich* that I think bears noting in this regard. It is a statement that Hill imagined coming from Thomas Edison, who was part of Hill's "imaginary counsel," as described above. Hill and Edison did, in fact, have brief correspondence. Shortly before the publication of Hill's first book *The Law of Success* in 1928, he sent the inventor his manuscript; Edison replied that he had time to give it only a "cursory examination," but from what he read he believed "your philosophy is sound . . . if your students of this philosophy will work as hard in applying it as you have in building it they will be amply rewarded for their labor." Coming from the pen of Edison, that's creditable praise. The following statement, as noted, came not from Edison but from Hill's imaginary dialogue with him. I find it a good summary of Hill's perspective, and, for its era, a reasonable attempt at describing the physics of the Master Mind:

One evening Edison arrived ahead of all the others. He walked over and seated himself at my left, where Emerson was accustomed to sit, and said, "You are destined to witness the discovery of the secret of life. When the time comes, you will observe that life consists of great swarms of energy, or entities, each as intelligent as human beings *think* themselves to be. These units of life group together like hives of bees, and remain together until they disintegrate, *through lack of harmony*. These units have differences of opinion, the same as human beings, and often fight among themselves. These meetings which you are conducting will be very helpful to you. They will bring to your rescue some of the same units of life which served the members of your Cabinet, during their lives. These units are eternal. THEY NEVER DIE! Your own thoughts and DESIRES serve as the magnet which attracts units of life, from the great ocean of life out there. Only the friendly units are attracted— the ones which harmonize with the nature of your DESIRES."

The other members of the Cabinet began to enter the room. Edison got up, and slowly walked around to his own seat. Edison was still living when this happened. It impressed me so greatly that I went to see him, and told him about the experience. He smiled broadly, and said, "Your dream was more a reality than you may imagine it to have been." He added no further explanation to his statement.

Q: It is okay to be in touch with members in between meetings?

A: Of course. People in your group may be friends or workmates, or may be collaborating on a project together. Do not be overly formal about group contacts. It is perfectly natural, and expected, that members may check in or get together during interim periods. The Master Mind strengthens your personal bonds—it does not proscribe them. Feel free to carry on your natural friendships and relationships in between meetings. It is fine for Master Minders to provide advice, support, and guidance to one another in or out of meetings, if the mutual desire exists. But always make sure that the group is robust—never form cliques or tale-bear about other members.

Q: Under what circumstances is it okay to miss a meeting? What if I'm traveling, sick, or on vacation?

A: Life is complex, and we're all going to miss a meeting once in a while. But I would make every effort, even during travel or while experiencing a minor illness, to be at your meeting or call. If you want the Master Mind to be there for you, you must be there for it. Steadiness of attendance and regular participation lend consistency and potency to your group's efforts; there is no substitute for showing up. Participation also builds trust. You may be relaxing on vacation, or traveling in a different time zone and feeling off-schedule, but a fellow member may be in need—and hearing your voice and counsel could be the very thing that pulls him through. This kind of consistency strengthens everyone's faith, and the stock they place in the Master Mind, which ultimately aids all members.

Q: Can I raise personal issues in my Master Mind group?
A: Yes. In my group, we have discussed marital and relationship issues, emotional health, stress, childrearing, and any number of personal issues, in addition to career and professional matters. These topics often flow together. As the Master Mind principles state, the group's concerns encompass anything that relates to a "success-filled and happy life," including deeply personal matters. I wouldn't necessarily suggest venturing into such things in your first meeting or two—you might want to establish a sense of group familiarity and rapport before covering personal matters. But if your group has been well assembled, that intimacy will arrive quickly. You should feel at liberty to share any life issue with your Master Mind partners.

Q: You said that I should discuss my plans only with valid experts and members of my Master Mind group—but what about a spouse, best friend, or close family member?
A: Of course you can talk with intimate relations, such as a spouse. Think of your plans as a health question that you would share with close family members and specialists—but not just anyone. The point is not to cultivate isolation, or to be withholding, but rather to be discrete. Your Master Mind group plays a key role in this.

Afterword

A Master Mind for Everyone

"For where two or three are gathered in my name,
I am there with them."
—MATTHEW 20:18

In writing this exhortation to form and maintain a Master Mind group, I realize that for some readers this may be temporarily impossible. For reasons beyond your control, you may be, for the time being, unable find a second person with whom to start a group, or you may be facing other barriers. Do not worry. There is an option for you.

What I am about to offer is *not* a substitute for the Master Mind, but rather an augmentation to it, and a bridge during those times when you find it unworkable to gather with others. You can gather silently with me.

Each day at 3 p.m. eastern standard time (EST), I enter into a short period of prayer and reflection. Christian tradition sometimes teaches that 3 p.m. is when Christ died on the cross. A popular Catholic devotion terms it "The Hour of Great Mercy." It is a period when people everywhere (varying by differences in time zone) pause in prayer, silent unity, and good intentions. This time is used not only for personal wishes, but also for wishing others well, perhaps praying for someone's recovery from illness—or any worthy thing needed in your life, or that of a friend, colleague, or loved one.

I set a permanent daily alarm on my phone for 3 p.m. EST, and suggest that you do the same. No matter where you are—on an elevator, in a meeting, even driving (as long as you don't take eyes off the road)—you can pause from your onrush of thoughts to express gratitude, meditate on ethical wishes, and think on things that are of good and productive purpose. We can do this together at 3 p.m. EST, or you can do it on your own, or with others in your time zone.

I invite you to join me each day in this silent compact—a kind of Master Mind across whatever hours and geography separate us. Remember: this practice cannot replace a Master Mind. Think of it simply as a long-distance fellowship, and a bridge until you can enter into a traditional Master Mind arrangement. I vow to you that, barring a medical emergency or some other urgency, I will be with you each day at 3 p.m. EST in reflection and prayer.

I cannot personally know all of you who are reading these words; but I will hold a wish at that hour for the highest ethical attainments of all who join in, and ask that you do the same.

ACTION STEP:
"I Ask Not For More Blessings"

I have long admired this prayer from Napoleon Hill, which you may want to recite daily. If it speaks to you, write it down on a card and keep it readily at hand:

I ask not for more blessings, but more wisdom with which to make better use of the blessings I now possess. And give me, please, more understanding that I may occupy more space in the hearts of my fellow men by rendering more service tomorrow than I have rendered today.

Feel free to address the prayer to God, Infinite Intelligence (as Hill sometimes did), or use it simply as a meditation that speaks to your highest ideals.

Appendix I

The Over-Soul:
Inner Key to the Master Mind

At the back of Hill's concept of the Master Mind is Ralph Waldo Emerson's exploration of "The Over-Soul." As Emerson notes in his seminal 1841 essay, there exists a Higher Mind, or what Hill called Infinite Intelligence, in which all beings dwell, and whose insights flow through you at your most sensitive moments.

The more you are traversed by ideas of this higher creative Mind, which is the source of all that is, the more natural, truthful, beneficent, and efficacious are your ideas. At such moments, ideas cease to be merely "yours" and are, rather, expressions of Truth, in its ultimate sense.

The entire project of the Master Mind, in its fullest realization, is to bring participants in contact with Infinite Intelligence. The genius of Hill's program is that, in addition to its practical, motivational, and educational qualities, its methods place you in the stream of universal laws and ethics. As such, you are in service to your highest development, and that of others'.

Your Master Mind alliance is a *means* of experiencing Infinite Intelligence or the Over-Soul. Remember this next time you feel too "busy" to make time for your group meeting. You are not only in a compact with your partners, but, ideally, with the highest source of all ideas.

Below you will find full text of "The Over-soul," as Emerson published it in his *First Series* of essays, along with my commentary, in which I punctuate those points that are especially pertinent to the Master Mind. This great statement of Emerson's is one of the clearest, plainest, most unadorned expressions of how you relate to the higher principle of life. It reveals your state of mind when you're in touch with Infinite Intelligence. I think you will return to this essay for the rest of your life.

For his part, Napoleon Hill wrote about Emerson with veneration, and the philosopher's ideas motivated Hill early in his search. The Master Mind grew from Hill's mission to find concrete techniques that open you to universal insights and natural laws. As you read Emerson's essay, you will recognize antecedents behind some of Hill's ideas. As a piece of writing, "The Over-soul" will seem at once familiar and startlingly fresh. You may encounter patches of arcane or inscrutable language; do not worry: push past them and their meaning will quickly become clear—Emerson often capped his ideas with a phrase or line of resounding clarity.

My annotations are meant to elucidate and highlight core ideas, and relate them back to the aims of this book and your Master Mind efforts. In some cases, I have commented in the middle of Emerson's paragraphs, in other cases at the end. His original paragraphs are demarcated by indentations.

The Over-Soul

"But souls that of his own good life partake,
He loves as his own self; dear as his eye
They are to Him: He'll never them forsake:
When they shall die, then God himself shall die:
They live, they live in blest eternity."
—*Henry More*

Space is ample, east and west,
But two cannot go abreast,
Cannot travel in it two:
Yonder masterful cuckoo
Crowds every egg out of the nest,
Quick or dead, except its own;
A spell is laid on sod and stone,
Night and Day've been tampered with,
Every quality and pith
Surcharged and sultry with a power
That works its will on age and hour.

There is a difference between one and another hour of life, in their authority and subsequent effect. Our faith comes in moments; our vice is habitual.

MH: Emerson is identifying the human situation: You are granted highest perspective—but only at your most exceptional moments of sensitivity, and departures from habit and routine.

Yet there is a depth in those brief moments which constrains us to ascribe more reality to them than to all other experiences. For this reason, the argument which is always forthcoming to silence those who conceive extraordinary hopes of man, namely, the appeal to experience, is for ever invalid and vain. We give up the past to the objector, and yet we hope. He must explain this hope. We grant that human life is mean; but how did we find out that it was mean? What is the ground of this uneasiness of ours; of this old discontent? What is the universal sense of want and ignorance, but the fine inuendo by which the soul makes its enormous claim? Why do men feel that the natural history of man has never been written, but he is always leaving behind what you have said of him, and it becomes old, and books of metaphysics worthless?

MH: Your discontent with the ordinary, and your experience of sublime moments of life, validates the existence of something greater. Such greater moments are reference points of and testimony to highest truth, by which the rest of life is measured.

The philosophy of six thousand years has not searched the chambers and magazines of the soul. In its experiments there has always remained, in the last analysis, a residuum it could not resolve. Man is a stream whose source is hidden. Our being is descending into us from we know not whence. The most exact calculator has no prescience that somewhat incalculable may not balk the very next moment. I am constrained every moment to acknowledge a higher origin for events than the will I call mine.

MH: The sublime is realer than the routine. True life and authentic insights emanate from this higher quality.

As with events, so is it with thoughts. When I watch that flowing river, which, out of regions I see not, pours for a season its streams into me, I see that I am a pensioner; not a cause, but a surprised spectator of this ethereal water; that I desire and look up, and put myself in the attitude of reception, but from some alien energy the visions come.

MH: You understand so little of the nature of true insight and perception. In your most sensitive moments, however, you see hazily that it originates from a greater source.

The Supreme Critic on the errors of the past and the present, and the only prophet of that which must be, is that great nature in which we rest, as the earth lies in the soft arms of the atmosphere; that Unity, that Over-soul, within which every man's particular being is contained and made one with all other; that common heart, of which all sincere conversation is the worship, to which all right action is submission; that overpowering reality which confutes our tricks and talents, and constrains every one to pass for what he is, and to speak from his character, and not from his tongue, and which evermore tends to pass into our thought and hand, and become wisdom, and virtue, and power, and beauty. We live in succession, in division, in parts, in particles. Meantime within man is the soul of the whole; the wise silence; the universal beauty, to which every part and particle is equally related; the eternal ONE.

MH: You live in fragments, but you are part of a greater whole: the Over-Soul, or what Hill calls the Master Mind and Infinite Intelligence. This is what makes you, at your highest moments, authentic and original in your thought and speech, rather than just a chamber of echo and repetition.

And this deep power in which we exist, and whose beatitude is all accessible to us, is not only self-sufficing and perfect in every hour, but the act of seeing and the thing seen, the seer and the spectacle, the subject and the object, are one. We see the world piece by piece, as the sun, the moon, the animal, the tree; but the whole, of which these are the shining parts, is the soul. Only by the vision of that Wisdom can the horoscope of the ages be read, and by falling back on our better thoughts, by yielding to the spirit of prophecy which is innate in every man, we can know what it saith. Every man's words, who speaks from that life, must sound vain to those who do not dwell in the same thought on their own part. I dare not speak for it. My words do not carry its august sense; they fall short and cold. Only itself can inspire whom it will, and behold! their speech shall be lyrical, and sweet, and universal as the rising of the wind. Yet I desire, even by profane words, if I may not use sacred, to indicate the heaven of this deity, and to report what hints I have collected of the transcendent simplicity and energy of the Highest Law.

MH: Your ideas and insights emerge from a pool of higher thought. When you function with authority and grace, you are subject to, and perceptive of, this higher principle of life, which undergirds all that you are.

If we consider what happens in conversation, in reveries, in remorse, in times of passion, in surprises, in the instructions of dreams, wherein often we see ourselves in masquerade,—the droll disguises only magnifying and enhancing a real element, and forcing it on our distinct notice,—we shall catch many hints that will broaden and lighten into knowledge of the secret of nature. All goes to show that the soul in man is not an organ, but animates and exercises all the organs; is not a function, like the power of memory, of calculation, of comparison, but uses these as hands and feet; is not a faculty, but a light; is not the intellect or the will, but the master of the intellect and the will; is the background of our being, in which they lie,—an immensity not possessed and that cannot be possessed.

MH: The soul within you is not a result or a faculty, but the cause of all results and faculties. You must be receptive to its influence. The more open, the higher and the greater you may be. The absence of the soul's influence reduces you to imitation and mimicry.

From within or from behind, a light shines through us upon things, and makes us aware that we are nothing, but the light is all. A man is the fasade of a temple wherein all wisdom and all good abide. What we commonly call man, the eating, drinking, planting, counting man, does not, as we know him, represent himself, but misrepresents himself. Him we do not respect, but the soul, whose organ he is, would he let it appear through his action, would make our knees bend. When it breathes through his intellect, it is genius; when it breathes through his will, it is virtue; when it flows through his affection, it is love. And the blindness of the intellect begins, when it would be something of itself. The weakness of the will begins, when the individual would be something of himself. All reform aims, in some one particular, to let the soul have its way through us; in other words, to engage us to obey.

MH: All brilliance, all originality, all constructiveness, and all virtue—all self-development—occur when there is *less* of the particular self, and more of the Higher traversing through you. You more fully evince what is vital, lasting, and real when you are receptive. Can you get out of the way and allow higher causes, or Infinite Intelligence, to operate through you?

Of this pure nature every man is at some time sensible. Language cannot paint it with his colors. It is too subtile. It is undefinable, unmeasurable, but we know that it pervades and contains us. We know that all spiritual being is in man. A wise old proverb says, "God comes to see us without bell"; that is, as there is no screen or ceiling between our heads and the infinite heavens, so is there no bar or wall in the soul where man, the effect, ceases, and God, the cause, begins. The walls are taken away. We lie open on one side to the deeps of spiritual nature, to the attributes of God. Justice we see and know, Love, Freedom, Power. These natures no man ever got above, but they tower over us, and most in the moment when our interests tempt us to wound them.

MH: The individual is an effect of the Higher; but the personality obfuscates the True.

The sovereignty of this nature whereof we speak is made known by its independency of those limitations which circumscribe us on every hand. The soul circumscribes all things. As I have said, it contradicts all experience. In like manner it abolishes time and space. The influence of the senses has, in most men, overpowered the mind to that degree, that the walls of time and space have come to look real and insurmountable; and to speak with levity of these limits is, in the world, the sign of insanity. Yet time and space are but inverse measures of the force of the soul. The spirit sports with time,—"Can crowd eternity into an hour, Or stretch an hour to eternity."

MH: You believe only in outer forms, and not the reality from which they spring. Yet the reality that undergirds them is the Truth.

We are often made to feel that there is another youth and age than that which is measured from the year of our natural birth. Some thoughts always find us young, and keep us so. Such a thought is the love of the universal and eternal beauty. Every man parts from that contemplation with the feeling that it rather belongs to ages than to mortal life. The least activity of the intellectual powers redeems us in a degree from the conditions of time. In sickness, in languor, give us a strain of poetry, or a profound sentence, and we are refreshed; or produce a volume of Plato, or Shakspeare, or remind us of their names, and instantly we come into a feeling of longevity. See how the deep, divine thought reduces centuries, and millenniums, and makes itself present through all ages. Is the teaching of Christ less effective now than it was when first his mouth was opened? The emphasis of facts and persons in my thought has nothing to do with time. And so, always, the soul's scale is one; the scale of the senses and the understanding is another. Before the revelations of the soul, Time, Space, and Nature shrink away. In common speech, we refer all things to time, as we habitually refer the immensely sundered stars to one concave sphere. And so we say that the Judgment is distant or near, that the Millennium approaches, that a day of certain political, moral, social reforms is at hand, and the like, when we mean, that, in the nature of things, one of the facts we contemplate is external and fugitive, and the other is permanent and connate with the soul. The things we now esteem fixed shall, one by one, detach themselves, like ripe fruit, from our experience, and fall. The wind shall blow them none knows whither. The landscape, the figures, Boston, London, are facts as fugitive as any institution past, or any whiff of mist or smoke, and so is society, and so is the world. The soul looketh steadily forwards, creating a world before her, leaving worlds behind her. She has no dates, nor rites, nor persons, nor specialties, nor men. The soul knows only the soul; the web of events is the flowing robe in which she is clothed.

MH: High revelations disrupt our sense of time and order. Feelings and sensations may then flow unimpeded from our limited concepts of what is possible. Truth is dateless, boundless, and unfenced by culture or condition. It is universal and always urgent.

After its own law and not by arithmetic is the rate of its progress to be computed. The soul's advances are not made by gradation, such as can be represented by motion in a straight line; but rather by ascension of state, such as can be represented by metamorphosis,— from the egg to the worm, from the worm to the fly. The growths of genius are of a certain *total* character, that does not advance the elect individual first over John, then Adam, then Richard, and give to each the pain of discovered inferiority, but by every throe of growth the man expands there where he works, passing, at each pulsation, classes, populations, of men. With each divine impulse the mind rends the thin rinds of the visible and finite, and comes out into eternity, and inspires and expires its air. It converses with truths that have always been spoken in the world, and becomes conscious of a closer sympathy with Zeno and Arrian, than with persons in the house.

MH: All minds are One. You are not a local being. You realize this when you partake of the Higher Mind.

This is the law of moral and of mental gain. The simple rise as by specific levity, not into a particular virtue, but into the region of all the virtues. They are in the spirit which contains them all. The soul requires purity, but purity is not it; requires justice, but justice is not that; requires beneficence, but is somewhat better; so that there is a kind of descent and accommodation felt when we leave speaking of moral nature, to urge a virtue which it enjoins. To the well-born child, all the virtues are natural, and not painfully acquired. Speak to his heart, and the man becomes suddenly virtuous.

MH: All virtues are merely translations of Divine experience. The Over-Soul, or Infinite Intelligence, is higher and simpler than all outer expressions. The Over-Soul translates into virtues, of which It is the original source. Virtues themselves cannot replicate the Creative Force of which they are a shadow expression.

Within the same sentiment is the germ of intellectual growth, which obeys the same law. Those who are capable of humility, of justice, of love, of aspiration, stand already on a platform that commands the sciences and arts, speech and poetry, action and grace. For whoso dwells in this moral beatitude already anticipates those special powers which men prize so highly. The lover has no talent, no skill, which passes for quite nothing with his enamoured maiden, however little she may possess of related faculty; and the heart which abandons itself to the Supreme Mind finds itself related to all its works, and will travel a royal road to particular knowledges and powers. In ascending to this primary and aboriginal sentiment, we have come from our remote station on the circumference instantaneously to the centre of the world, where, as in the closet of God, we see causes, and anticipate the universe, which is but a slow effect.

MH: The Supreme Mind is the primal substance of all that is. The closer you approach It, the greater and more far-reaching are your works.

One mode of the divine teaching is the incarnation of the spirit in a form,—in forms, like my own. I live in society; with persons who answer to thoughts in my own mind, or express a certain obedience to the great instincts to which I live. I see its presence to them. I am certified of a common nature; and these other souls, these separated selves, draw me as nothing else can.

MH: Others are drawn to, feel affection for, and obey the appearance of our common nature, as it exists and emanates from the Divine Mind.

They stir in me the new emotions we call passion; of love, hatred, fear, admiration, pity; thence comes conversation, competition, persuasion, cities, and war. Persons are supplementary to the primary teaching of the soul. In youth we are mad for persons. Childhood and youth see all the world in them. But the larger experience of man discovers the identical nature appearing through them all. Persons themselves acquaint us with the impersonal. In all conversation between two persons, tacit reference is made, as to a third party, to a common nature. That third party or common nature is not social; it is impersonal; is God.

MH: At sensitive moments, you recognize that you are a mere extension or reflection of the Higher, as are all who you experience.

And so in groups where debate is earnest, and especially on high questions, the company become aware that the thought rises to an equal level in all bosoms, that all have a spiritual property in what was said, as well as the sayer. They all become wiser than they were.

MH: The constructive exchange that occurs within a group can elevate all who participate. This is the core of Hill's claim for the Master Mind. You can also see this in his description of the signers of the Declaration of Independence.

It arches over them like a temple, this unity of thought, in which every heart beats with nobler sense of power and duty, and thinks and acts with unusual solemnity. All are conscious of attaining to a higher self-possession. It shines for all. There is a certain wisdom of humanity which is common to the greatest men with the lowest, and which our ordinary education often labors to silence and obstruct. The mind is one, and the best minds, who love truth for its own sake, think much less of property in truth. They accept it thankfully everywhere, and do not label or stamp it with any man's name, for it is theirs long beforehand, and from eternity. The learned and the studious of thought have no monopoly of wisdom. Their violence of direction in some degree disqualifies them to think truly.

MH: All individuals are vessels; none is greater than the other; all that matters is how open a conduit you are so that the finest influences may traverse and flow through you. The learned sometimes learn and act by rote, and are less authentic for that.

We owe many valuable observations to people who are not very acute or profound, and who say the thing without effort, which we want and have long been hunting in vain. The action of the soul is oftener in that which is felt and left unsaid, than in that which is said in any conversation. It broods over every society, and they unconsciously seek for it in each other. We know better than we do. We do not yet possess ourselves, and we know at the same time that we are much more. I feel the same truth how often in my trivial conversation with my neighbours, that somewhat higher in each of us overlooks this by-play, and Jove nods to Jove from behind each of us.

MH: God is not known in you by your achievements or social banter. In fact, too much of one's individual achievement or worldly artifice can conceal the Higher. But at the back of all human relations, the Higher Presence is *felt*.

Men descend to meet. In their habitual and mean service to the world, for which they forsake their native nobleness, they resemble those Arabian sheiks, who dwell in mean houses, and affect an external poverty, to escape the rapacity of the Pacha, and reserve all their display of wealth for their interior and guarded retirements.

MH: Custom, rank, privilege, and other social devices *conceal* our shared and innate glory.

As it is present in all persons, so it is in every period of life. It is adult already in the infant man. In my dealing with my child, my Latin and Greek, my accomplishments and my money stead me nothing; but as much soul as I have avails. If I am wilful, he sets his will against mine, one for one, and leaves me, if I please, the degradation of beating him by my superiority of strength. But if I renounce my will, and act for the soul, setting that up as umpire between us two, out of his young eyes looks the same soul; he reveres and loves with me.

MH: Not when you coerce or force, but when you discover the holy commonality between yourself and another do justice and right action naturally appear.

The soul is the perceiver and revealer of truth. We know truth when we see it, let skeptic and scoffer say what they choose. Foolish people ask you, when you have spoken what they do not wish to hear, 'How do you know it is truth, and not an error of your own?' We know truth when we see it, from opinion, as we know when we are awake that we are awake.

MH: Forget pedantic truths and the game-playing arguments of men. You *know* Truth. (In this vein, Hill repeatedly cautioned against opinion or hearsay.)

It was a grand sentence of Emanuel Swedenborg, which would alone indicate the greatness of that man's perception,—"It is no proof of a man's understanding to be able to confirm whatever he pleases; but to be able to discern that what is true is true, and that what is false is false, this is the mark and character of intelligence." In the book I read, the good thought returns to me, as every truth will, the image of the whole soul. To the bad thought which I find in it, the same soul becomes a discerning, separating sword, and lops it away. We are wiser than we know. If we will not interfere with our thought, but will act entirely, or see how the thing stands in God, we know the particular thing, and every thing, and every man. For the Maker of all things and all persons stands behind us, and casts his dread omniscience through us over things.

MH: You possess a soul-certain confidence when you are in the presence of Truth. The Higher recognizes itself. When you thus speak, you are unchallenged; your grasp of truth is self-evident. When you do a thing, do all of it in Truth. Not in fragments—but follow the whole arc of Truth.

But beyond this recognition of its own in particular passages of the individual's experience, it also reveals truth. And here we should seek to reinforce ourselves by its very presence, and to speak with a worthier, loftier strain of that advent. For the soul's communication of truth is the highest event in nature, since it then does not give somewhat from itself, but it gives itself, or passes into and becomes that man whom it enlightens; or, in proportion to that truth he receives, it takes him to itself.

MH: Do not seek to *express* truth; rather, *live* truth. It is unmistakable. It is not a byproduct, an opinion, or a case—it is Truth itself. "We are wiser than we know."

We distinguish the announcements of the soul, its manifestations of its own nature, by the term *Revelation*. These are always attended by the emotion of the sublime. For this communication is an influx of the Divine mind into our mind.

MH: The philosopher and mystic Emanuel Swedenborg (1688-1772), who Emerson quoted above, wrote of a "Divine influx" into the individual. This is a central idea found in recovery groups—although sometimes in different language—and in the Master Mind alliance when Hill writes of members being a pathway for Infinite Intelligence.

It is an ebb of the individual rivulet before the flowing surges of the sea of life. Every distinct apprehension of this central commandment agitates men with awe and delight. A thrill passes through all men at the reception of new truth, or at the performance of a great action, which comes out of the heart of nature. In these communications, the power to see is not separated from the will to do, but the insight proceeds from obedience, and the obedience proceeds from a joyful perception. Every moment when the individual feels himself invaded by it is memorable. By the necessity of our constitution, a certain enthusiasm attends the individual's consciousness of that divine presence. The character and duration of this enthusiasm varies with the state of the individual, from an ecstasy and trance and prophetic inspiration,—which is its rarer appearance,—to the faintest glow of virtuous emotion, in which form it warms, like our household fires, all the families and associations of men, and makes society possible. A certain tendency to insanity has always attended the opening of the religious sense in men, as if they had been "blasted with excess of light." The trances of Socrates, the "union" of Plotinus, the vision of Porphyry, the conversion of Paul, the aurora of Behmen, the convulsions of George Fox and his Quakers, the illumination of Swedenborg, are of this kind. What was in the case of these remarkable persons a ravishment has, in innumerable instances in common life, been exhibited in less striking manner. Everywhere the history of religion betrays a tendency to enthusiasm. The rapture of the Moravian and Quietist; the opening of the internal sense of the Word, in the language of the New Jerusalem Church; the *revival* of the Calvinistic churches; the *experiences* of the Methodists, are varying forms of that shudder of awe and delight with which the individual soul always mingles with the universal soul.

MH: The revelation of truth always comes as a sensational experience. Sometimes it is a quiet knowing. Other times it is rapturous, exuberant, and physically ecstatic. Whatever the expression, it is an experience of knowing and *being*—not claiming or insisting.

The nature of these revelations is the same; they are perceptions of the absolute law. They are solutions of the soul's own questions. They do not answer the questions which the understanding asks. The soul answers never by words, but by the thing itself that is inquired after.

MH: Truth is not a position or a formulation; it *is*.

Revelation is the disclosure of the soul. The popular notion of a revelation is, that it is a telling of fortunes. In past oracles of the soul, the understanding seeks to find answers to sensual questions, and undertakes to tell from God how long men shall exist, what their hands shall do, and who shall be their company, adding names, and dates, and places. But we must pick no locks. We must check this low curiosity. An answer in words is delusive; it is really no answer to the questions you ask. Do not require a description of the countries towards which you sail. The description does not describe them to you, and to-morrow you arrive there, and know them by inhabiting them. Men ask concerning the immortality of the soul, the employments of heaven, the state of the sinner, and so forth. They even dream that Jesus has left replies to precisely these interrogatories. Never a moment did that sublime spirit speak in their *patois*.

MH: No real truth is local or situational, or found in fortunetelling or forecasting. The smallness of your hourly concerns and low ambitions can never fully contain or convey Truth.

To truth, justice, love, the attributes of the soul, the idea of immutableness is essentially associated. Jesus, living in these moral sentiments, heedless of sensual fortunes, heeding only the manifestations of these, never made the separation of the idea of duration from the essence of these attributes, nor uttered a syllable concerning the duration of the soul. It was left to his disciples to sever duration from the moral elements, and to teach the immortality of the soul as a doctrine, and maintain it by evidences. The moment the doctrine of the immortality is separately taught, man is already fallen. In the flowing of love, in the adoration of humility, there is no question of continuance. No inspired man ever asks this question, or condescends to these evidences. For the soul is true to itself, and the man in whom it is shed abroad cannot wander from the present, which is infinite, to a future which would be finite.

MH: Doctrines are debased substitutes for dwelling in the presence of the Whole.

These questions which we lust to ask about the future are a confession of sin. God has no answer for them. No answer in words can reply to a question of things.

MH: God speaks in principles, not occurrences.

It is not in an arbitrary "decree of God," but in the nature of man, that a veil shuts down on the facts of to-morrow; for the soul will not have us read any other cipher than that of cause and effect. By this veil, which curtains events, it instructs the children of men to live in to-day. The only mode of obtaining an answer to these questions of the senses is to forego all low curiosity, and, accepting the tide of being which floats us into the secret of nature, work and live, work and live, and all unawares the advancing soul has built and forged for itself a new condition, and the question and the answer are one.

MH: Natural ethics are the ruler of life. We are not given to see the future because that is not seeing into Truth. Conditions are not set in conformity—but rather they live and unfold as we come to know truth, principle, and inner refinement.

By the same fire, vital, consecrating, celestial, which burns until it shall dissolve all things into the waves and surges of an ocean of light, we see and know each other, and what spirit each is of. Who can tell the grounds of his knowledge of the character of the several individuals in his circle of friends? No man. Yet their acts and words do not disappoint him. In that man, though he knew no ill of him, he put no trust. In that other, though they had seldom met, authentic signs had yet passed, to signify that he might be trusted as one who had an interest in his own character. We know each other very well,— which of us has been just to himself, and whether that which we teach or behold is only an aspiration, or is our honest effort also.

MH: Character is the only barometer of life. It shines through you in such a manner that it cannot be concealed for long.

We are all discerners of spirits. That diagnosis lies aloft in our life or unconscious power. The intercourse of society,—its trade, its religion, its friendships, its quarrels,—is one wide, judicial investigation of character. In full court, or in small committee, or confronted face to face, accuser and accused, men offer themselves to be judged. Against their will they exhibit those decisive trifles by which character is read. But who judges? and what? Not our understanding. We do not read them by learning or craft. No; the wisdom of the wise man consists herein, that he does not judge them; he lets them judge themselves, and merely reads and records their own verdict.

MH: Evidence of worth comes not from details or pedantry but from how a thing or person comports with Higher Nature. This can always be felt.

By virtue of this inevitable nature, private will is overpowered, and, maugre our efforts or our imperfections, your genius will speak from you, and mine from me. That which we are, we shall teach, not voluntarily, but involuntarily.

MH: All behavior, attitudes, and actions, both public and private, are justly compensated and known.

Thoughts come into our minds by avenues which we never left open, and thoughts go out of our minds through avenues which we never voluntarily opened. Character teaches over our head. The infallible index of true progress is found in the tone the man takes. Neither his age, nor his breeding, nor company, nor books, nor actions, nor talents, nor all together, can hinder him from being deferential to a higher spirit than his own. If he have not found his home in God, his manners, his forms of speech, the turn of his sentences, the build, shall I say, of all his opinions, will involuntarily confess it, let him brave it out how he will. If he have found his centre, the Deity will shine through him, through all the disguises of ignorance, of ungenial temperament, of unfavorable circumstance. The tone of seeking is one, and the tone of having is another.

MH: We pass for what we are—nothing can evade or alter natural perception. This statement of Emerson's should become the motto of our times, and the guiding compass of all that you post and read on social media: "The infallible index of true progress is found in the tone the man takes."

The great distinction between teachers sacred or literary,—between poets like Herbert, and poets like Pope,—between philosophers like Spinoza, Kant, and Coleridge, and philosophers like Locke, Paley, Mackintosh, and Stewart,—between men of the world, who are reckoned accomplished talkers, and here and there a fervent mystic, prophesying, half insane under the infinitude of his thought,—is, that one class speak *from within*, or from experience, as parties and possessors of the fact; and the other class, *from without*, as spectators merely, or perhaps as acquainted with the fact on the evidence of third persons. It is of no use to preach to me from without. I can do that too easily myself. Jesus speaks always from within, and in a degree that transcends all others. In that is the miracle. I believe beforehand that it ought so to be. All men stand continually in the expectation of the appearance of such a teacher. But if a man do not speak from within the veil, where the word is one with that it tells of, let him lowly confess it.

MH: The truly great speak from who they *are*, not from what they observe or judge.

The same Omniscience flows into the intellect, and makes what we call genius. Much of the wisdom of the world is not wisdom, and the most illuminated class of men are no doubt superior to literary fame, and are not writers. Among the multitude of scholars and authors, we feel no hallowing presence; we are sensible of a knack and skill rather than of inspiration; they have a light, and know not whence it comes, and call it their own; their talent is some exaggerated faculty, some overgrown member, so that their strength is a disease. In these instances the intellectual gifts do not make the impression of virtue, but almost of vice; and we feel that a man's talents stand in the way of his advancement in truth. But genius is religious. It is a larger imbibing of the common heart. It is not anomalous, but more like, and not less like other men. There is, in all great poets, a wisdom of humanity which is superior to any talents they exercise. The author, the wit, the partisan, the fine gentleman, does not take place of the man. Humanity shines in Homer, in Chaucer, in Spenser, in Shakspeare, in Milton. They are content with truth. They use the positive degree. They seem frigid and phlegmatic to those who have been spiced with the frantic passion and violent coloring of inferior, but popular writers. For they are poets by the free course which they allow to the informing soul, which through their eyes beholds again, and blesses the things which it hath made. The soul is superior to its knowledge; wiser than any of its works. The great poet makes us feel our own wealth, and then we think less of his compositions. His best communication to our mind is to teach us to despise all he has done. Shakspeare carries us to such a lofty strain of intelligent activity, as to suggest a wealth which beggars his own; and we then feel that the splendid works which he has created, and which in other hours we extol as a sort of self-existent poetry, take no stronger hold of real nature than the shadow of a passing traveller on the rock. The inspiration which uttered itself in Hamlet and Lear could utter things as good from day to day, for ever. Why, then, should I make account of Hamlet and Lear, as if we had not the soul from which they fell as syllables from the tongue?

MH: Great art does not arise through skill or artifice, but through the degree of truth that permeates its messenger. You then forget the artist and the work, and witness only Truth.

This energy does not descend into individual life on any other condition than entire possession.

MH: You cannot be partially awake.

It comes to the lowly and simple; it comes to whomsoever will put off what is foreign and proud; it comes as insight; it comes as serenity and grandeur. When we see those whom it inhabits, we are apprized of new degrees of greatness. From that inspiration the man comes back with a changed tone. He does not talk with men with an eye to their opinion. He tries them. It requires of us to be plain and true. The vain traveller attempts to embellish his life by quoting my lord, and the prince, and the countess, who thus said or did to *him*. The ambitious vulgar show you their spoons, and brooches, and rings, and preserve their cards and compliments. The more cultivated, in their account of their own experience, cull out the pleasing, poetic circumstance,—the visit to Rome, the man of genius they saw, the brilliant friend they know; still further on, perhaps, the gorgeous landscape, the mountain lights, the mountain thoughts, they enjoyed yesterday,—and so seek to throw a romantic color over their life. But the soul that ascends to worship the great God is plain and true; has no rose-color, no fine friends, no chivalry, no adventures; does not want admiration; dwells in the hour that now is, in the earnest experience of the common day,—by reason of the present moment and the mere trifle having become porous to thought, and bibulous of the sea of light.

MH: Greatness seeks not to impress, accumulate, or gather endorsements. It presents nothing but itself. It questions; it weighs; it does not curry favor or make pleas.

Converse with a mind that is grandly simple, and literature looks like word-catching. The simplest utterances are worthiest to be written, yet are they so cheap, and so things of course, that, in the infinite riches of the soul, it is like gathering a few pebbles off the ground, or bottling a little air in a phial, when the whole earth and the whole atmosphere are ours. Nothing can pass there, or make you one of the circle, but the casting aside your trappings, and dealing man to man in naked truth, plain confession, and omniscient affirmation.

MH: Avoid pith and cleverness. Do not try to catch lightning in a bottle.

Souls such as these treat you as gods would; walk as gods in the earth, accepting without any admiration your wit, your bounty, your virtue even,—say rather your act of duty, for your virtue they own as their proper blood, royal as themselves, and over-royal, and the father of the gods. But what rebuke their plain fraternal bearing casts on the mutual flattery with which authors solace each other and wound themselves! These flatter not. I do not wonder that these men go to see Cromwell, and Christina, and Charles the Second, and James the First, and the Grand Turk. For they are, in their own elevation, the fellows of kings, and must feel the servile tone of conversation in the world. They must always be a godsend to princes, for they confront them, a king to a king, without ducking or concession, and give a high nature the refreshment and satisfaction of resistance, of plain humanity, of even companionship, and of new ideas. They leave them wiser and superior men. Souls like these make us feel that sincerity is more excellent than flattery. Deal so plainly with man and woman, as to constrain the utmost sincerity, and destroy all hope of trifling with you. It is the highest compliment you can pay. Their "highest praising," said Milton, "is not flattery, and their plainest advice is a kind of praising."

MH: Truth is naturally magnetic. Earth's materially great seek the company of individuals in whom authenticity dwells; they consider them equals—and more. People tire of flattery but never of natural sincerity.

Ineffable is the union of man and God in every act of the soul. The simplest person, who in his integrity worships God, becomes God; yet for ever and ever the influx of this better and universal self is new and unsearchable. It inspires awe and astonishment. How dear, how soothing to man, arises the idea of God, peopling the lonely place, effacing the scars of our mistakes and disappointments! When we have broken our god of tradition, and ceased from our god of rhetoric, then may God fire the heart with his presence. It is the doubling of the heart itself, nay, the infinite enlargement of the heart with a power of growth to a new infinity on every side. It inspires in man an infallible trust. He has not the conviction, but the sight, that the best is the true, and may in that thought easily dismiss all particular uncertainties and fears, and adjourn to the sure revelation of time, the solution of his private riddles. He is sure that his welfare is dear to the heart of being. In the presence of law to his mind, he is overflowed with a reliance so universal, that it sweeps away all cherished hopes and the most stable projects of mortal condition in its flood. He believes that he cannot escape from his good. The things that are really for thee gravitate to thee. You are running to seek your friend. Let your feet run, but your mind need not. If you do not find him, will you not acquiesce that it is best you should not find him? for there is a power, which, as it is in you, is in him also, and could therefore very well bring you together, if it were for the best. You are preparing with eagerness to go and render a service to which your talent and your taste invite you, the love of men and the hope of fame. Has it not occurred to you, that you have no right to go, unless you are equally willing to be prevented from going? O, believe, as thou livest, that every sound that is spoken over the round world, which thou oughtest to hear, will vibrate on thine ear! Every proverb, every book, every byword that belongs to thee for aid or comfort, shall surely come home through open or winding passages. Every friend whom not thy fantastic will, but the great and tender heart in thee craveth, shall lock thee in his embrace. And this, because the heart in thee is the heart of all; not a valve, not a wall, not an intersection is there anywhere in nature, but one blood rolls uninterruptedly an endless circulation through all men, as the water of the globe is all one sea, and, truly seen, its tide is one.

MH: That which is naturally yours comes to you. You cannot heighten affections, hasten an appointment, or force an engagement—at least not for long. As water finds its natural level, so do circumstances and relations that are rightly yours reach you.

Let man, then, learn the revelation of all nature and all thought to his heart; this, namely; that the Highest dwells with him; that the sources of nature are in his own mind, if the sentiment of duty is there. But if he would know what the great God speaketh, he must 'go into his closet and shut the door,' as Jesus said. God will not make himself manifest to cowards. He must greatly listen to himself, withdrawing himself from all the accents of other men's devotion. Even their prayers are hurtful to him, until he have made his own.

MH: You must be willing to receive what is rightly yours; and just as willing to lose what is not. Live in Truth.

Our religion vulgarly stands on numbers of believers. Whenever the appeal is made—no matter how indirectly—to numbers, proclamation is then and there made, that religion is not. He that finds God a sweet, enveloping thought to him never counts his company. When I sit in that presence, who shall dare to come in? When I rest in perfect humility, when I burn with pure love, what can Calvin or Swedenborg say?

MH: Greatness is not in numbers, popularity, or prestige—it dwells within you when your heart beats fearlessly and joyfully in rhythm with Truth.

It makes no difference whether the appeal is to numbers or to one. The faith that stands on authority is not faith. The reliance on authority measures the decline of religion, the withdrawal of the soul. The position men have given to Jesus, now for many centuries of history, is a position of authority. It characterizes themselves. It cannot alter the eternal facts. Great is the soul, and plain. It is no flatterer, it is no follower; it never appeals from itself. It believes in itself. Before the immense possibilities of man, all mere experience, all past biography, however spotless and sainted, shrinks away. Before that heaven which our presentiments foreshow us, we cannot easily praise any form of life we have seen or read of. We not only affirm that we have few great men, but, absolutely speaking, that we have none; that we have no history, no record of any character or mode of living, that entirely contents us. The saints and demigods whom history worships we are constrained to accept with a grain of allowance. Though in our lonely hours we draw a new strength out of their memory, yet, pressed on our attention, as they are by the thoughtless and customary, they fatigue and invade. The soul gives itself, alone, original, and pure, to the Lonely, Original, and Pure, who, on that condition, gladly inhabits, leads, and speaks through it. Then is it glad, young, and nimble. It is not wise, but it sees through all things. It is not called religious, but it is innocent. It calls the light its own, and feels that the grass grows and the stone falls by a law inferior to, and dependent on, its nature. Behold, it saith, I am born into the great, the universal mind. I, the imperfect, adore my own Perfect. I am somehow receptive of the great soul, and thereby I do overlook the sun and the stars, and feel them to be the fair accidents and effects which change and pass. More and more the surges of everlasting nature enter into me, and I become public and human in my regards and actions. So come I to live in thoughts, and act with energies, which are immortal. Thus revering the soul, and learning, as the ancient said, that "its beauty is immense," man will come to see that the world is the perennial miracle which the soul worketh, and be less astonished at particular wonders; he will learn that there is no profane history; that all history is sacred; that the universe is represented in an atom, in a moment of time. He will weave no longer a spotted life of shreds and patches, but he will live with a divine unity. He will cease from what is base and frivolous in his life, and be content with all places and with any service he can render. He will calmly front the morrow in the negligency of that trust which carries God with it, and so hath already the whole future in the bottom of the heart.

MH: True authority does not come from law. True greatness does not come from valorous examples, or in the particular works of men. It exists above all these. Greatness dwells in the heart of a simple, translucent, God-aspiring individual—who, in high moments, partakes of all that is.

Appendix II

The Sixteen Laws of Success

There are sixteen laws of success: these traits can be found in the life of nearly any exceptional person. Each Napoleon Hill Success Course goes into detail about one or more of these laws. Although it is important to master all sixteen principles, the traits of the whole are, in a sense, inherent in each one, the same way a primeval forest may be traced back to a solitary acorn.

1. DEFINITE CHIEF AIM. The starting point of all achievement is having a definite, passionate, and specific aim. This is no ordinary desire, but something you're willing to dedicate your life to. It must be written down, read daily, acted upon constantly, and held in your heart with total commitment.

2. **THE MASTER MIND**. As you've been reading, this is a harmonious alliance ranging from as few as two to as many as seven people who meet at regular intervals to exchange ideas, advice, and sometimes meditations and prayers for one another's success. The Master Mind is critical to your plans, as the pooling of intellects results in a sum greater than the parts.

3. **SELF-CONFIDENCE**. You must possess or develop confidence to push on with your plans. If have low self-confidence, you can bolster it through meditations, visualizations, autosuggestion, and the Master Mind.

4. **INITIATIVE AND LEADERSHIP**. Leadership is essential to success—and initiative is the foundation upon which leadership stands. Initiative means *doing what ought to be done without being told to*. Only those who practice initiative become leaders.

5. **IMAGINATION**. In order to have a *definite purpose, self-confidence, initiative* and *leadership*, you must first create these qualities in your *imagination*, and see them as yours. Imagination is the visualizing faculty that lays out your plans, and connects knowledge with ideas.

6. **ENTHUSIASM**. This is the vital ingredient that allows you to get things done. Without enthusiasm, nothing is possible. With it, you demonstrate acts of tireless commitment, which sometimes seem

miraculous. This is why is your aim must tap your passions. Enthusiasm is the closest thing to a magic elixir.

7.   **SELF-CONTROL**. Self-control is the force through which your enthusiasm is directed toward constructive ends. Without self-control—of speech, actions, and thought—enthusiasm is like unharnessed lightening: it may strike anywhere. The successful person possesses both *enthusiasm* and *self-control*.

8.   **DOING MORE THAN PAID FOR**. You are most efficient, and will more quickly and easily succeed, when dedicated to work that you love. When you work with passion, the quality and quantity of your work improve, and you naturally do more and better work than you are paid for. This is why you owe it to yourself to find the work you like best.

9.   **PLEASING PERSONALITY**. Your personality is the sum total of your characteristics and appearance: the clothes you wear, your facial expressions, the vitality of your body, your handshake, your tone of voice, your thoughts, and most importantly *the character you have developed by those thoughts.*

10.   **ORGANIZED PLANNING**. You must form definite, well-researched, and practical plans for enacting and seeing through your desires. It is imperative to begin acting on your plans immediately, even if in a small way. This relates to the following step.

11.   ACCURATE THOUGHT. Accurate thought is vital
      to success. Thinking accurately means relying on
      facts, observations, experience, and data that are
      relevant to your aim. This means shunning gossip,
      rumor, hearsay, idle talk, and casual opinions.

12.   CONCENTRATION. The more you concentrate
      upon your goal the more you benefit from the
      law of autosuggestion, through which persistent,
      emotionally charged ideas impress your
      subconscious, and organize your thoughts and
      energies in the service of your definite chief aim.
      Concentration is a form of power.

13.   COOPERATION. Success cannot be attained
      singlehandedly. It requires cooperative effort. If
      your work is based upon cooperation rather than
      competition, you will get places faster and enjoy
      an additional reward in happiness. To win the
      cooperation of others you must offer them a strong
      motive or reward.

14.   PROFITING BY FAILURE. What we call failure is
      often temporary defeat. Temporary defeat frequently
      proves a blessing because it jolts us and redirects
      our energies along more desirable paths. Reversals,
      setbacks, and temporary defeat impel the success-
      drive person toward improved character and plans.

15.   TOLERANCE. Intolerance, bigotry, hostile sarcasm,
      and bullying make enemies; they disintegrate the
      organized forces of society; they substitute mob

psychology in place of reason. These forces must be mastered before enduring success may be attained.

16. THE GOLDEN RULE. Your thoughts and actions set in motion a power that runs its course in the lives of others, returning, finally, to help or hinder you. This law is immutable—but you can adapt yourself to it and use it as an irresistible force that will carry you to achievement. You do this through living at all times, as best you are able, by the Golden Rule.

About Napoleon Hill

NAPOLEON HILL was born in 1883 in Wise County, Virginia. He worked as a secretary, a reporter for a local newspaper, the manager of a coalmine and a lumberyard, and attended law school, before taking a job as a journalist for *Bob Taylor's Magazine,* an inspirational and general-interest journal. In 1908, Hill interviewed steel magnate Andrew Carnegie who told him that success could be distilled into a set of practical principles. The industrialist urged Hill to interview high achievers in every field to discover these principles. Hill dedicated himself to this study for more than twenty years, and distilled what he found into his books *The Law of Success* (1928), *Think and Grow Rich* (1937), and other classic works. Hill spent the rest of his life documenting and refining the principles of success. After a career as an author, publisher, lecturer, and business consultant, the motivational pioneer died in 1970 in South Carolina. Learn more about Napoleon Hill and the Napoleon Hill Foundation at www.NapHill.org.

About Mitch Horowitz

One of today's most literate voices in self-help, MITCH HOROWITZ is a PEN Award-winning historian and the author of books including *Occult America; The Miracle Club: How Thoughts Become Reality; One Simple Idea: How Positive Thinking Reshaped Modern Life*; and *The Miracle of a Definite Chief Aim*, the first book in the Napoleon Hill Success Course Series. Mitch has written on everything from the war on witches to the secret life of Ronald Reagan for *The New York Times, The Wall Street Journal, Politico, Salon,* and *Time. The Washington Post* says Mitch "treats esoteric ideas and movements with an even-handed intellectual studiousness that is too often lost in today's raised-voice discussions." Mitch narrates audio books including *Alcoholics Anonymous, The Jefferson Bible,* and G&D Media's Condensed Classics series. He is a monthly columnist for *Science of Mind* magazine and lecturer-in-residence at the University of Philosophical Research in Los Angeles. Visit him at www.MitchHorowitz.com and @MitchHorowitz.